PYTHON DATA VISUALIZATION

Create Stunning Data Visualizations with Python Libraries

THOMPSON CARTER

TABLE OF CONTENTS

Introduction

In a world increasingly driven by data, the ability to present complex information visually and effectively has never been more critical. Data visualization is not just an art but a science—one that bridges the gap between raw data and actionable insights. It empowers individuals and organizations to explore patterns, communicate findings, and make informed decisions. Whether it's a line chart tracking financial growth, a heatmap revealing geographic trends, or a 3D plot illustrating intricate relationships, data visualization brings numbers to life.

This book, ***Python Data Visualization: Create Stunning Data Visualizations with Python Libraries***, serves as a comprehensive guide for anyone looking to master the craft of data storytelling using Python. Designed to be accessible, practical, and jargon-free, this book combines the power of Python's robust visualization libraries with real-world examples, helping readers translate data into impactful visuals.

Why Data Visualization Matters

In the digital age, data is abundant and pervasive. From tracking global climate trends to monitoring social media engagement, the insights buried within datasets are vast but often hidden. Data visualization solves this challenge by transforming abstract numbers into visual forms that are intuitive and meaningful. It allows individuals to:

1. **Discover Insights**: Spot trends, correlations, and outliers that might be missed in raw data.
2. **Communicate Effectively**: Share findings with stakeholders in a way that is easily understood, even by non-technical audiences.
3. **Drive Action**: Facilitate decision-making by presenting data in a compelling and persuasive manner.

However, creating effective visualizations requires more than technical know-how. It demands an understanding of design principles, audience needs, and the ability to tell a story through visuals.

Why Python for Data Visualization?

Python has emerged as one of the most popular programming languages for data science and analytics, thanks to its versatility and an extensive ecosystem of libraries. For data visualization, Python offers tools ranging from simple plotting utilities to sophisticated, interactive dashboards.

Key reasons to choose Python for data visualization include:

1. **Comprehensive Libraries**:
   o **Matplotlib**: The foundational library for creating static, publication-quality plots.
   o **Seaborn**: Built on top of Matplotlib, it simplifies creating visually appealing statistical graphics.
   o **Plotly**: Enables interactive and dynamic visualizations, perfect for web and exploratory analysis.
   o **Other Specialized Tools**: Libraries like Bokeh, Geopandas, and Folium cater to niche visualization needs.
2. **Integration with Data Science Workflows**: Python seamlessly integrates data preprocessing, analysis, and visualization, creating a unified workflow.
3. **Flexibility and Customization**: Python's libraries allow for an unparalleled degree of customization, enabling users to create tailored visuals that align with specific requirements.
4. **Community Support**: The Python ecosystem boasts a vast and active community, providing tutorials, documentation, and support for visualization enthusiasts.

Who Is This Book For?

This book is designed for a broad audience, including:

- **Beginners**: Those new to data visualization will find step-by-step instructions and simple examples to build foundational skills.
- **Data Analysts and Scientists**: Professionals looking to enhance their ability to communicate insights through visuals.
- **Students and Academics**: Researchers aiming to present findings effectively in reports and publications.
- **Business Professionals**: Individuals seeking to create compelling dashboards and presentations to support decision-making.

Whether you're an experienced programmer or a novice learning Python for the first time, this book caters to your needs by starting with the basics and gradually progressing to advanced topics.

What to Expect from This Book

This book is structured to provide a comprehensive journey through the world of Python-based data visualization, from foundational concepts to cutting-edge trends. Here's a snapshot of what you'll learn:

1. **Foundations**: Understand the principles of data visualization, including chart selection, color theory, and audience considerations.
2. **Core Libraries**: Master essential libraries like Matplotlib, Seaborn, and Plotly, learning their capabilities and how to use them effectively.
3. **Specialized Techniques**: Explore techniques for visualizing geospatial data, networks, time series, and more.
4. **Interactivity and Dashboards**: Build dynamic, interactive dashboards that allow users to explore data in real time.
5. **Real-World Applications**: Apply visualization techniques to domains like business analytics, health, environmental science, and social media.
6. **Emerging Trends**: Discover the future of data visualization with AI-powered tools, augmented reality, and real-time analytics.

What Makes This Book Unique?

Unlike many technical books that focus heavily on syntax and code, this book emphasizes the **why** behind each visualization technique. You'll not only learn how to create visualizations but also understand when and why to use specific charts or tools. Real-world examples and exercises are woven throughout, ensuring that the concepts are practical and immediately applicable.

Additionally, this book focuses on:

1. **Jargon-Free Explanations**: Complex ideas are presented in plain language, making them accessible to all readers.
2. **Hands-On Learning**: Every chapter includes detailed examples and exercises to reinforce learning.
3. **Aesthetic and Functional Visuals**: The book emphasizes both the design and technical aspects of visualization, ensuring that your visuals are not only accurate but also visually compelling.

A Call to Action

Data visualization is more than a technical skill; it's a critical form of communication in today's data-driven world. By mastering the techniques in this book, you'll not only enhance your ability to work with data but also amplify your ability to tell stories, influence decisions, and drive change.

Whether you're presenting findings to stakeholders, conducting academic research, or exploring data for personal curiosity, this book is your companion on the journey to creating stunning, impactful visualizations.

Let's begin the journey to bring data to life!

Chapter 1: Introduction to Data Visualization

Overview

Data visualization is the practice of presenting data in a visual format, enabling individuals and organizations to understand patterns, trends, and outliers quickly. This chapter provides an in-depth understanding of the importance, guiding principles, and transformative potential of data visualization across various domains.

Key Objectives

At the end of this chapter, you will:

1. Recognize the role of data visualization in decision-making and communication.
2. Learn the foundational principles of creating effective visualizations.
3. Examine real-world examples where data visualization has created impact.

Section 1: Why Data Visualization Matters

1.1 Bridging the Gap Between Data and Understanding

- Data is ubiquitous, but raw numbers lack meaning without context.
- Visualization is a tool that decodes data into actionable insights.
  - o **Example**: Visualizing millions of sales records as a trend line helps identify growth or decline over time.

1.2 Enhancing Human Cognition Through Visualization

- **How the Brain Processes Visual Information**:
  - o Visuals leverage the brain's natural ability to detect patterns, making complex data digestible.
  - o **Fact**: 90% of the information transmitted to the brain is visual.
- **Real-World Case**:
  - o A logistics company visualizes delivery routes using heatmaps, reducing fuel costs by 20%.

1.3 Everyday Applications of Data Visualization

1. **Business**:
   - o Sales dashboards for tracking real-time performance.
   - o Example: Amazon's dashboard that monitors sales peaks during Prime Day.
2. **Healthcare**:

- COVID-19 dashboards tracking infection rates and vaccination progress.
- Visualization Example: Johns Hopkins University's global COVID-19 tracker.

3. **Science and Environment**:
   - Climate models that visualize rising temperatures or deforestation.

Section 2: Core Principles of Effective Data Visualization

2.1 Clarity: The Non-Negotiable Factor

- Avoid overloading visuals with excessive data points.
  - **Good Example**: A pie chart with three categories.
  - **Bad Example**: A pie chart with 20 slices—confusing and ineffective.
- Simplify complex data while retaining meaning.
  - **Technique**: Group smaller categories under "Other" for clarity.

2.2 Know Your Audience

- Tailoring visualizations for different audiences ensures relevance.
  - **Executives**: High-level insights like KPIs or trends.

- o **Technical Teams**: Detailed charts with granular data points.
- **Case Study**:
  - o A tech company presenting data to investors used clean bar charts, while internal teams received detailed scatter plots.

2.3 Accuracy in Representation

- Misleading visuals can distort decision-making:
  - o **Example of Failure**:
    - A news outlet used a truncated y-axis to exaggerate differences in polling data.
  - o **Guideline**: Always start the y-axis at zero unless context requires otherwise.

2.4 Context is Key

- Provide the context to avoid misinterpretation.
  - o Annotate key data points on line graphs.
  - o Use descriptive titles, legends, and labels.

Section 3: The Real-World Impact of Visualization

3.1 Driving Business Insights

- **Case Study: Walmart's Data-Driven Decision-Making**
  - Walmart used heatmaps to optimize store layouts, increasing revenue by 12%.
  - **Visual Used**: A heatmap of in-store foot traffic.

3.2 Visualizations in Storytelling

- Data visualizations enhance storytelling, creating emotional connections with viewers.
  - **Example**: A nonprofit organization showing the impact of donations through a before-and-after chart.
- **Interactive Tools**: Using Tableau or Power BI to create dashboards that allow stakeholders to explore data narratives interactively.

3.3 Identifying Trends and Anomalies

- Time-series visualizations for stock market trends help investors make informed decisions.
- Outlier detection in visualizations highlights areas requiring immediate attention, such as sudden sales drops.

Chapter Summary

- **The Why**: Data visualization is essential for turning raw data into actionable insights.
- **The How**: Core principles like clarity, audience focus, and accuracy form the foundation of effective visualization.
- **The Impact**: From business to healthcare, visualization drives decision-making and fosters understanding.

Exercise: Reflect and Apply

1. **Analyze**: Look at a chart or graph from a recent news article. Is it clear and accurate? What would you improve?
2. **Create**: Using a dataset (e.g., COVID-19 statistics, sales data), design a simple line chart that communicates a key insight.
3. **Feedback**: Share your visualization with a peer. Ask:
   o Is it easy to understand?
   o Does it tell a clear story?

Chapter 2: Getting Started with Python for Data Visualization

Overview

Before diving into data visualization techniques, it's essential to have the right tools and environment set up. This chapter introduces Python as the preferred programming language for data visualization, explains how to install and configure necessary tools, and provides an overview of key libraries and IDEs that facilitate data visualization.

Key Objectives

By the end of this chapter, readers will:

1. Understand why Python is a powerful tool for data visualization.
2. Learn how to install and configure Python and its essential libraries.
3. Explore the various IDEs available for coding and visualization.

Section 1: Why Python for Data Visualization?

2.1 Python's Popularity and Community Support

- Python is one of the most widely used languages for data science and visualization.
- Advantages include:
  - o Extensive library support (Matplotlib, Seaborn, Plotly, etc.).
  - o Easy-to-learn syntax for beginners.
  - o A large community for troubleshooting and tutorials.

2.2 Real-World Applications of Python in Visualization

- **Business**: Dashboards and reports (e.g., sales trends).
- **Science**: Visualization of experimental data.
- **Web Development**: Interactive charts integrated into websites.

Section 2: Setting Up Python for Visualization

2.3 Installing Python

- Step-by-step instructions for installation:
  - o Windows: Download from python.org.
  - o MacOS: Pre-installed on most systems but should be updated.

o Linux: Use package managers like apt or yum.

2.4 Installing Essential Libraries

- Use pip to install libraries:

bash

pip install numpy pandas matplotlib seaborn plotly

- Brief description of each library:
    - **Numpy**: Efficient numerical operations.
    - **Pandas**: Data manipulation and cleaning.
    - **Matplotlib**: Core visualization library.
    - **Seaborn**: Statistical data visualization built on Matplotlib.
    - **Plotly**: Interactive and dynamic visualizations.

2.5 Setting Up a Virtual Environment

- Benefits:
    - Avoid conflicts between library versions.
    - Maintain separate environments for different projects.
- Commands to create and activate a virtual environment:

bash

```
python -m venv env
source env/bin/activate  # For Mac/Linux
.\env\Scripts\activate  # For Windows
```

Section 3: IDEs for Data Visualization

2.6 Overview of Popular IDEs

1. **Jupyter Notebook**:
   - Interactive environment for writing and running code.
   - Ideal for testing visualizations and documenting workflows.
   - Installation:

     bash

     pip install notebook

   - Example Workflow: Create a line chart in a Jupyter cell and see the output immediately.

2. **VS Code (Visual Studio Code)**:
   - Lightweight yet powerful editor with extensions for Python.
   - Setup: Install Python extension for autocomplete and debugging.

3. **PyCharm**:
   - Comprehensive IDE for larger Python projects.

- ○ Integrated tools for virtual environments and package management.

4. **Google Colab**:
   - ○ Cloud-based environment for running Python code.
   - ○ No installation required; perfect for quick testing and sharing.

2.7 Setting Up Your IDE

- **Jupyter Notebook Setup**:
  - ○ Install Jupyter and launch with:

    bash

    jupyter notebook

  - ○ Navigate to your working directory via the web interface.
- **VS Code Setup**:
  - ○ Install Python and Jupyter extensions.
  - ○ Configure the interpreter to point to your virtual environment.

Section 4: Testing Your Environment

2.8 Writing Your First Visualization Code

- Import necessary libraries and create a simple plot:

```python
python

import matplotlib.pyplot as plt

x = [1, 2, 3, 4, 5]
y = [2, 3, 5, 7, 11]

plt.plot(x, y)
plt.title("Sample Line Plot")
plt.xlabel("X-axis")
plt.ylabel("Y-axis")
plt.show()
```

- Test in your preferred IDE to ensure everything is working.

2.9 Debugging Common Issues

- Missing modules: Use pip install <module_name>.
- Python not recognized: Add Python to your system PATH during installation.
- IDE not recognizing virtual environment: Ensure the correct interpreter is selected.

Chapter Summary

- Python is an ideal choice for data visualization due to its robust libraries and community support.
- Setting up Python, libraries, and IDEs correctly is crucial for efficient workflows.
- Testing your environment ensures a smooth start to creating visualizations.

Exercise: Apply Your Setup

1. Install Python and the libraries mentioned in this chapter.
2. Choose an IDE and configure it for Python development.
3. Write and run the sample code to create a simple line plot.
4. Reflect: Which part of the setup was easiest? Which required troubleshooting?

Chapter 3: Data Preparation for Visualization

Overview

Effective data visualization starts with clean, well-structured data. Preparing data involves cleaning errors, transforming data formats, and understanding its structure and patterns to ensure accurate and meaningful visualizations. This chapter guides readers through essential techniques for preparing data for visualization, using Python's powerful data manipulation libraries.

Key Objectives

By the end of this chapter, readers will:

1. Understand why data preparation is crucial for visualization.
2. Learn techniques for cleaning and transforming data.
3. Use Python libraries to explore and understand data.

Section 1: Why Data Preparation is Important

3.1 The Role of Clean Data in Visualization

- Visualizations are only as good as the data behind them.

- Dirty data leads to:
    - Misleading insights.
    - Broken or unreadable visualizations.

3.2 Common Data Issues

1. **Missing Values**: Gaps in data can skew visualizations.
2. **Duplicate Entries**: Redundant rows can distort trends.
3. **Outliers**: Extreme values that may or may not represent errors.
4. **Inconsistent Formatting**: Different units, date formats, or naming conventions.

3.3 Example of Poor vs. Clean Data

- **Poor Data**: A sales dataset with missing months and inconsistent currency symbols.
- **Clean Data**: Gaps filled, consistent formats applied, ready for analysis.

Section 2: Cleaning Data

3.4 Removing Duplicates

- **Python Implementation**:

python

```
import pandas as pd

df = pd.DataFrame({
    'Name': ['Alice', 'Bob', 'Alice'],
    'Sales': [200, 150, 200]
})

df = df.drop_duplicates()
print(df)
```

3.5 Handling Missing Values

- Options:
    1. Drop rows/columns with missing values.
    2. Fill missing values with mean, median, or a constant.
- **Python Implementation**:

python

```
df['Sales'] = df['Sales'].fillna(df['Sales'].mean())
```

3.6 Standardizing Data Formats

- Convert inconsistent data to a standard format (e.g., dates, units).
- **Python Implementation**:

python

```
df['Date'] = pd.to_datetime(df['Date'])
```

3.7 Dealing with Outliers

- Detect outliers using statistical methods (e.g., Z-scores, IQR).
- **Example**: Removing outliers from a dataset.

python

```
df = df[(df['Sales'] > df['Sales'].quantile(0.05)) &
    (df['Sales'] < df['Sales'].quantile(0.95))]
```

Section 3: Transforming Data

3.8 Reshaping Data

- Pivot tables, stacking, and unstacking:
    - Wide to long format (or vice versa) depending on visualization needs.
    - **Python Implementation**:

      python

      ```
      df = df.pivot(index='Date', columns='Product', values='Sales')
      ```

3.9 Aggregating Data

- Group data by categories and calculate metrics like sums or averages.
- **Python Implementation**:

python

```
grouped = df.groupby('Category')['Sales'].sum()
print(grouped)
```

3.10 Merging and Joining Data

- Combine datasets for a comprehensive analysis.
- **Python Implementation**:

python

```
df1 = pd.DataFrame({'ID': [1, 2], 'Name': ['Alice', 'Bob']})
df2 = pd.DataFrame({'ID': [1, 2], 'Sales': [200, 150]})

merged = pd.merge(df1, df2, on='ID')
print(merged)
```

Section 4: Understanding Your Data

3.11 Exploring Data with Pandas

- View the structure and key statistics of your dataset:

python

```
print(df.head())  # First 5 rows
print(df.info())  # Dataset overview
print(df.describe())  # Statistical summary
```

3.12 Identifying Patterns

- Plot basic visualizations to identify trends or irregularities before diving deeper.
- Example:

python

```
import matplotlib.pyplot as plt

df['Sales'].plot(kind='line')
plt.show()
```

3.13 Case Study: Preparing Real-World Data

- Dataset: Sales data with missing dates, duplicate rows, and inconsistent units.
- Steps:
  1. Remove duplicates.
  2. Fill missing dates with interpolation.
  3. Standardize currency units to USD.
  4. Aggregate sales by month.

Chapter Summary

- Data preparation is a critical step for creating accurate visualizations.
- Cleaning involves handling missing values, duplicates, and inconsistencies.
- Transformation ensures data is in the right structure for visualization.
- Exploring data helps identify trends and informs visualization choices.

Exercise: Practice Cleaning and Transforming Data

1. Load a sample dataset with issues (e.g., missing values, duplicates).
2. Apply the techniques in this chapter to clean and transform it.
3. Create a basic line chart to verify the cleaned data is ready for visualization.

Chapter 4: Understanding Chart Types and Their Use Cases

Overview

Choosing the right chart type is essential for effectively conveying data insights. This chapter explores the most common chart types, their use cases, and practical tips for selecting the best one based on the data and intended message.

Key Objectives

By the end of this chapter, readers will:

1. Understand the most commonly used chart types.
2. Learn the scenarios where each chart type is most effective.
3. Be able to select the right chart to match their data and goals.

Section 1: The Importance of Choosing the Right Chart

4.1 The Role of Chart Selection in Communication

- An appropriate chart enhances clarity and understanding.
- The wrong chart can misrepresent data or confuse the audience.

4.2 Factors to Consider When Choosing a Chart

1. **Data Type**:
   - o Numerical, categorical, or temporal.
2. **Objective**:
   - o Comparison, distribution, relationship, or composition.
3. **Audience**:
   - o Technical experts may prefer detailed charts; general audiences need simplicity.

Section 2: Common Chart Types and Their Use Cases

4.3 Bar Charts

- **Purpose**: Compare quantities across categories.
- **When to Use**:
  - o Comparing sales across regions.
  - o Visualizing survey responses.
- **Variants**:
  - o Grouped bar charts for multiple categories.
  - o Stacked bar charts to show composition.
- **Example with Code**:

python

```
import matplotlib.pyplot as plt

categories = ['A', 'B', 'C']
values = [30, 70, 50]

plt.bar(categories, values)
plt.title("Bar Chart Example")
plt.xlabel("Categories")
plt.ylabel("Values")
plt.show()
```

4.4 Line Charts

- **Purpose**: Show trends over time.
- **When to Use**:
    - Stock market trends.
    - Website traffic over a week.
- **Variants**:
    - Multiple lines for comparing trends.
- **Example with Code**:

python

```
import matplotlib.pyplot as plt

time = ['Jan', 'Feb', 'Mar']
sales = [200, 220, 250]
```

```
plt.plot(time, sales)
plt.title("Line Chart Example")
plt.xlabel("Time")
plt.ylabel("Sales")
plt.show()
```

4.5 Scatter Plots

- **Purpose**: Explore relationships between two numerical variables.
- **When to Use**:
  - o Analyzing correlation between marketing spend and revenue.
  - o Detecting clusters or outliers.
- **Variants**:
  - o Bubble charts to add a third dimension.
- **Example with Code**:

python

```
import matplotlib.pyplot as plt

x = [1, 2, 3, 4]
y = [2, 4, 6, 8]

plt.scatter(x, y)
plt.title("Scatter Plot Example")
plt.xlabel("X-axis")
plt.ylabel("Y-axis")
```

```
plt.show()
```

4.6 Pie Charts

- **Purpose**: Show proportions of a whole.
- **When to Use**:
    o Visualizing budget allocation.
    o Representing market share.
- **Tips**:
    o Avoid using too many slices; it reduces clarity.
- **Example with Code**:

python

```
sizes = [20, 30, 50]
labels = ['Product A', 'Product B', 'Product C']

plt.pie(sizes, labels=labels, autopct='%1.1f%%')
plt.title("Pie Chart Example")
plt.show()
```

4.7 Heatmaps

- **Purpose**: Represent values in a matrix format using colors.
- **When to Use**:
    o Displaying correlation between variables.
    o Visualizing website click data.
- **Example with Code**:

```
python
```

```
import seaborn as sns
import numpy as np

data = np.random.rand(5, 5)
sns.heatmap(data, annot=True)
```

4.8 Histograms

- **Purpose**: Show the distribution of a single numerical variable.
- **When to Use**:
  - Visualizing age distribution.
  - Analyzing frequency of sales.
- **Example with Code**:

```
python
```

```
import matplotlib.pyplot as plt

data = [10, 20, 20, 30, 40, 40, 50]

plt.hist(data, bins=5)
plt.title("Histogram Example")
plt.xlabel("Ranges")
plt.ylabel("Frequency")
plt.show()
```

Section 3: Advanced and Interactive Charts

4.9 Bubble Charts

- **Purpose**: Add a third variable to scatter plots using bubble size.

4.10 Area Charts

- **Purpose**: Similar to line charts but emphasize magnitude.

4.11 Interactive Charts with Plotly

- **Purpose**: Allow users to interact with data (e.g., zooming, filtering).
- **Example**: Interactive scatter plot with Plotly.

Section 4: Choosing the Right Chart

4.12 Chart Selection Matrix

Objective	Recommended Chart
Compare categories	Bar chart, grouped bar chart
Show trends over time	Line chart, area chart

Objective	Recommended Chart
Show relationships	Scatter plot, bubble chart
Show proportions	Pie chart, donut chart
Show distribution	Histogram, box plot

4.13 Tips for Effective Chart Selection

- Simplicity is key; avoid clutter.
- Match the chart to the data and audience.

Chapter Summary

- Different chart types serve distinct purposes in data visualization.
- Bar, line, scatter, and pie charts are foundational; advanced charts like heatmaps and bubble charts provide additional insights.
- Selecting the right chart enhances communication and clarity.

Exercise: Practice Choosing and Creating Charts

1. Use a dataset (e.g., sales, website traffic, or survey results).
2. Identify 3 different insights you want to visualize.
3. Choose the most appropriate chart type for each insight and create it using Python.

Chapter 5: Mastering Matplotlib

Overview

Matplotlib is one of the most powerful and widely used libraries for creating static, animated, and interactive visualizations in Python. This chapter provides a deep dive into the basics of Matplotlib, how to create various types of plots, and how to customize them to suit your visualization needs.

Key Objectives

By the end of this chapter, readers will:

1. Understand the structure and components of a Matplotlib figure.
2. Learn to create different types of plots using Matplotlib.
3. Master customization techniques to make plots more informative and visually appealing.

Section 1: Understanding Matplotlib

5.1 Introduction to Matplotlib

- Developed as a Python alternative to MATLAB for data visualization.

- Capable of producing publication-quality figures in various formats.

5.2 Anatomy of a Matplotlib Figure

- **Figure**: The overall container for the plot.
- **Axes**: The area where data is plotted (can have multiple Axes in one Figure).
- **Axis**: The x-axis or y-axis of a plot.
- **Artist**: Everything visible on the plot (lines, text, markers, etc.).
- **Code Example**:

```python
import matplotlib.pyplot as plt

fig, ax = plt.subplots()
ax.plot([1, 2, 3], [4, 5, 6])
plt.show()
```

Section 2: Creating Basic Plots

5.3 Line Plots

- Ideal for visualizing trends over time or ordered data.
- **Code Example**:

python

```
plt.plot([1, 2, 3, 4], [10, 20, 25, 30])
plt.title("Line Plot Example")
plt.xlabel("X-axis")
plt.ylabel("Y-axis")
plt.show()
```

5.4 Bar Charts

- Useful for comparing categorical data.
- **Code Example**:

python

```
categories = ['A', 'B', 'C']
values = [10, 20, 15]

plt.bar(categories, values)
plt.title("Bar Chart Example")
plt.show()
```

5.5 Scatter Plots

- Show relationships between two variables.
- **Code Example**:

python

```
x = [1, 2, 3, 4]
y = [10, 20, 25, 30]
```

```
plt.scatter(x, y)
plt.title("Scatter Plot Example")
plt.xlabel("X-axis")
plt.ylabel("Y-axis")
plt.show()
```

5.6 Histograms

- Display frequency distributions of a single variable.
- **Code Example**:

python

```
data = [10, 20, 20, 30, 40, 40, 50]

plt.hist(data, bins=5)
plt.title("Histogram Example")
plt.xlabel("Ranges")
plt.ylabel("Frequency")
plt.show()
```

5.7 Pie Charts

- Represent proportions of a whole.
- **Code Example**:

python

```
sizes = [20, 30, 50]
labels = ['Category A', 'Category B', 'Category C']
```

```
plt.pie(sizes, labels=labels, autopct='%1.1f%%')
plt.title("Pie Chart Example")
plt.show()
```

Section 3: Customizing Plots

5.8 Adding Titles, Labels, and Legends

- Use plt.title(), plt.xlabel(), plt.ylabel(), and plt.legend() to provide context.
- **Code Example**:

python

```
plt.plot([1, 2, 3, 4], [10, 20, 25, 30], label="Line A")
plt.title("Customized Plot Example")
plt.xlabel("Time")
plt.ylabel("Value")
plt.legend()
plt.show()
```

5.9 Styling Plots

- Customize line styles, colors, and markers:

python

```
plt.plot([1, 2, 3], [4, 5, 6], color='red', linestyle='--', marker='o')
```

```
plt.title("Styled Line Plot")
plt.show()
```

5.10 Controlling Axes and Grid

- Modify axis limits and add grids for clarity:

python

```
plt.plot([1, 2, 3], [4, 5, 6])
plt.xlim(0, 4)
plt.ylim(3, 7)
plt.grid(True)
plt.title("Axis Control Example")
plt.show()
```

5.11 Annotating Plots

- Highlight specific points or trends:

python

```
plt.plot([1, 2, 3], [4, 5, 6])
plt.annotate('Important Point', xy=(2, 5), xytext=(2.5, 5.5),
        arrowprops=dict(facecolor='black', arrowstyle='->'))
plt.title("Annotation Example")
plt.show()
```

Section 4: Advanced Matplotlib Features

5.12 Subplots

- Create multiple plots in one figure:

python

```
fig, axs = plt.subplots(2, 2)
axs[0, 0].plot([1, 2, 3], [4, 5, 6])
axs[0, 1].bar(['A', 'B', 'C'], [10, 20, 15])
axs[1, 0].scatter([1, 2, 3], [4, 5, 6])
axs[1, 1].pie([20, 30, 50], labels=['A', 'B', 'C'])
plt.tight_layout()
plt.show()
```

5.13 Saving Figures

- Save your plots to a file for reports or presentations:

python

```
plt.plot([1, 2, 3], [4, 5, 6])
plt.savefig("example_plot.png", dpi=300)
plt.show()
```

Chapter Summary

- Matplotlib provides comprehensive tools for creating and customizing plots.

- Mastery of basic plots (line, bar, scatter, histogram, and pie) is foundational for effective data visualization.
- Advanced features like subplots, annotations, and styling enhance the clarity and impact of visualizations.

Exercise: Hands-On Practice

1. Create a line plot, bar chart, and scatter plot using Matplotlib.
2. Customize one of the plots with a title, labels, legend, and annotations.
3. Save your plot to a file and include it in a document or presentation.

Chapter 6: Exploring Seaborn for Statistical Data

Overview

Seaborn is a Python data visualization library built on Matplotlib, designed to create beautiful and informative statistical graphics with minimal effort. This chapter explores Seaborn's capabilities, focusing on its advanced visualization techniques, statistical tools, and customization options to simplify complex data analysis.

Key Objectives

By the end of this chapter, readers will:

1. Understand Seaborn's role in statistical data visualization.
2. Learn to create advanced plots like pair plots, heatmaps, and categorical plots.
3. Master customization and styling in Seaborn.

Section 1: Introduction to Seaborn

6.1 Why Use Seaborn?

- Simplifies complex visualizations compared to Matplotlib.

- Focuses on statistical visualizations with built-in functions for aggregation and regression.
- Seamlessly integrates with Pandas for handling DataFrames.

6.2 Installing Seaborn

- Installation command:

  bash

  pip install seaborn

- Importing Seaborn:

  python

  import seaborn as sns

Section 2: Basic Visualizations with Seaborn

6.3 Creating Simple Plots

- Example   Dataset: Seaborn provides built-in datasets like tips and iris.

  python

  import seaborn as sns
  import matplotlib.pyplot as plt

```
tips = sns.load_dataset("tips")
```

- **Scatter Plot**:

python

```
sns.scatterplot(x="total_bill", y="tip", data=tips)
plt.title("Scatter Plot of Tips vs. Total Bill")
plt.show()
```

- **Line Plot**:

python

```
sns.lineplot(x="size", y="tip", data=tips)
plt.title("Line Plot of Tips by Party Size")
plt.show()
```

Section 3: Advanced Statistical Visualizations

6.4 Pair Plots

- Visualize relationships between all numeric variables in a dataset.
- **Code Example**:

python

```python
sns.pairplot(tips)
plt.show()
```

- Use hue for categorical separation:

python

```python
sns.pairplot(tips, hue="sex")
plt.show()
```

6.5 Heatmaps

- Represent correlation matrices or other matrix data.
- **Code Example**:

python

```python
correlation = tips.corr()
sns.heatmap(correlation, annot=True, cmap="coolwarm")
plt.title("Heatmap of Correlations")
plt.show()
```

6.6 Box Plots

- Summarize distributions and detect outliers.
- **Code Example**:

python

```python
sns.boxplot(x="day", y="total_bill", data=tips)
plt.title("Box Plot of Total Bill by Day")
```

```
plt.show()
```

6.7 Violin Plots

- Combine box plots and kernel density estimates.
- **Code Example**:

python

```
sns.violinplot(x="day", y="total_bill", data=tips, hue="sex", split=True)
plt.title("Violin Plot of Total Bill by Day and Gender")
plt.show()
```

6.8 Categorical Plots

- Compare categorical data with numeric data:
    o Bar plots: Aggregated metrics like mean or sum.

python

```
sns.barplot(x="day", y="total_bill", data=tips)
plt.title("Bar Plot of Total Bill by Day")
plt.show()
```

    o Count plots: Frequency of categories.

python

```
sns.countplot(x="day", data=tips)
plt.title("Count Plot of Days")
plt.show()
```

6.9 Regression Plots

- Show linear relationships between two variables.
- **Code Example**:

  python

  ```
  sns.regplot(x="total_bill", y="tip", data=tips)
  plt.title("Regression Plot of Tips vs. Total Bill")
  plt.show()
  ```

Section 4: Customizing Seaborn Visualizations

6.10 Changing Color Palettes

- Predefined palettes like coolwarm, viridis, and deep.
- **Code Example**:

  python

  ```
  sns.set_palette("coolwarm")
  sns.boxplot(x="day", y="total_bill", data=tips)
  plt.title("Box Plot with Custom Palette")
  plt.show()
  ```

6.11 Adjusting Themes

- Seaborn themes: darkgrid, whitegrid, dark, white, and ticks.
- **Code Example**:

python

```
sns.set_theme(style="whitegrid")
sns.scatterplot(x="total_bill", y="tip", data=tips)
plt.title("Scatter Plot with Whitegrid Theme")
plt.show()
```

6.12 Combining Seaborn and Matplotlib

- Add annotations or titles using Matplotlib functions:

python

```
ax = sns.boxplot(x="day", y="total_bill", data=tips)
ax.set_title("Box Plot with Matplotlib Title")
plt.xlabel("Day of the Week")
plt.ylabel("Total Bill")
plt.show()
```

Section 5: Case Study – Statistical Visualization with Seaborn

6.13 Dataset: Analyzing Employee Salaries

1. Load a CSV dataset with columns like Department, Salary, and Experience.

2. Steps:

   o Create a violin plot of Salary by Department.

- o Generate a heatmap showing correlations between Salary, Experience, and Age.
- o Use a regression plot to analyze the relationship between Salary and Experience.

Chapter Summary

- Seaborn simplifies statistical data visualization with intuitive functions and built-in themes.
- Advanced plots like pair plots, heatmaps, and violin plots provide deeper insights into complex datasets.
- Customization options and integration with Matplotlib make Seaborn versatile for any visualization need.

Exercise: Practice with Seaborn

1. Load the tips dataset or a dataset of your choice.
2. Create at least three different plots (e.g., heatmap, violin plot, pair plot).
3. Customize the plots with themes, palettes, and annotations.
4. Save the plots to files for use in reports or presentations.

Chapter 7: The Power of Pandas for Quick Visualizations

Overview

Pandas, a powerful library for data manipulation, also provides built-in capabilities for quick and effective visualizations. This chapter explores how to visualize data directly from Pandas DataFrames, offering convenience and speed for exploratory data analysis.

Key Objectives

By the end of this chapter, readers will:

1. Understand how to leverage Pandas for basic visualizations.
2. Create plots directly from DataFrames and Series.
3. Combine Pandas visualizations with Matplotlib for further customization.

Section 1: Introduction to Pandas Visualizations

7.1 Why Use Pandas for Visualization?

- Simplifies the workflow by integrating visualization directly into the data manipulation process.
- Provides quick insights during exploratory data analysis (EDA).
- Built on top of Matplotlib, allowing additional customization.

7.2 Setting Up for Pandas Visualizations

- Ensure Pandas and Matplotlib are installed:

bash

pip install pandas matplotlib

- Import the libraries:

python

import pandas as pd
import matplotlib.pyplot as plt

Section 2: Creating Visualizations Directly from DataFrames

7.3 Line Plots

- Useful for visualizing trends over time.

- **Code Example**:

python

```
data = {
    "Month": ["Jan", "Feb", "Mar", "Apr"],
    "Sales": [200, 220, 250, 270]
}
df = pd.DataFrame(data)

df.plot(x="Month", y="Sales", kind="line", title="Monthly Sales Trend")
plt.show()
```

7.4 Bar Charts

- Compare categorical data.
- **Code Example**:

python

```
data = {
    "Region": ["North", "South", "East", "West"],
    "Profit": [5000, 7000, 3000, 4000]
}
df = pd.DataFrame(data)

df.plot(x="Region", y="Profit", kind="bar", title="Profit by Region")
plt.show()
```

7.5 Histogram

- Analyze the frequency distribution of a single variable.
- **Code Example**:

python

```
df = pd.DataFrame({"Age": [22, 25, 30, 30, 40, 45, 50, 55, 60, 65]})

df["Age"].plot(kind="hist", bins=5, title="Age Distribution")
plt.show()
```

7.6 Scatter Plots

- Explore relationships between two numerical variables.
- **Code Example**:

python

```
data = {
    "Marketing Spend": [500, 700, 800, 1000],
    "Revenue": [7000, 9000, 11000, 15000]
}
df = pd.DataFrame(data)

df.plot(x="Marketing    Spend",    y="Revenue",    kind="scatter",
title="Marketing Spend vs. Revenue")
plt.show()
```

7.7 Pie Charts

- Show proportions of categories.

- **Code Example**:

    python

    ```
    data = {"Products": ["A", "B", "C"], "Market Share": [50, 30, 20]}
    df = pd.DataFrame(data)

    df.set_index("Products")["Market          Share"].plot(kind="pie",
    autopct="%1.1f%%", title="Market Share by Product")
    plt.ylabel("")  # Hide the y-label
    plt.show()
    ```

Section 3: Combining Pandas and Matplotlib

7.8 Customizing Pandas Plots with Matplotlib

- Add titles, labels, and legends:

    python

    ```
    df.plot(x="Month", y="Sales", kind="line")
    plt.title("Sales Over Time")
    plt.xlabel("Month")
    plt.ylabel("Sales")
    plt.grid(True)
    plt.show()
    ```

7.9 Multiple Series in One Plot

- Compare multiple variables:

python

```
data = {
    "Month": ["Jan", "Feb", "Mar", "Apr"],
    "Product A": [200, 220, 250, 270],
    "Product B": [150, 180, 200, 220]
}
df = pd.DataFrame(data)

df.plot(x="Month", y=["Product A", "Product B"], kind="line", title="Sales Comparison")
plt.show()
```

Section 4: Advanced Pandas Visualization Techniques

7.10 Grouped Data Visualization

- Aggregate and plot grouped data:

python

```
data = {
    "Region": ["North", "North", "South", "South"],
    "Sales": [5000, 7000, 8000, 6000],
    "Year": [2022, 2023, 2022, 2023]
}
df = pd.DataFrame(data)
```

```
grouped = df.groupby("Year")["Sales"].sum()
grouped.plot(kind="bar", title="Total Sales by Year")
plt.show()
```

7.11 Visualizing Time Series Data

- Use the Pandas datetime module for time-indexed data:

python

```
import pandas as pd
import matplotlib.pyplot as plt

data = {
    "Date": pd.date_range(start="2023-01-01", periods=5, freq="D"),
    "Visitors": [100, 150, 200, 250, 300]
}
df = pd.DataFrame(data)

df.plot(x="Date", y="Visitors", kind="line", title="Daily Visitors")
plt.show()
```

Section 5: Case Study – Visualizing Sales Data

7.12 Dataset: Monthly Sales and Profit

- Load a CSV dataset with columns like Month, Sales, and Profit.
- Steps:

1. Plot a line chart showing sales trends over time.
2. Create a bar chart comparing profit across regions.
3. Use a scatter plot to analyze the relationship between marketing spend and revenue.

Chapter Summary

- Pandas offers convenient, built-in visualization tools for quick insights during EDA.
- Common plot types include line charts, bar charts, histograms, scatter plots, and pie charts.
- Combining Pandas with Matplotlib enhances customization and clarity.

Exercise: Practice with Pandas Visualizations

1. Load a dataset using Pandas (e.g., sales, weather, or demographic data).
2. Create at least three different types of visualizations directly from the DataFrame.
3. Customize one plot with Matplotlib for enhanced clarity.
4. Reflect: How did visualizing data directly from Pandas streamline your analysis?

Chapter 8: Interactive Visualizations with Plotly

Overview

Plotly is a powerful Python library for creating interactive and dynamic visualizations. Unlike static charts, interactive visualizations allow users to zoom, pan, hover, and filter data, making it easier to explore complex datasets. This chapter introduces Plotly's core features and demonstrates how to create engaging, interactive charts.

Key Objectives

By the end of this chapter, readers will:

1. Understand the benefits of interactive visualizations.
2. Create interactive charts like line plots, bar charts, scatter plots, and dashboards using Plotly.
3. Explore customization and advanced features to enhance interactivity.

Section 1: Introduction to Plotly

8.1 Why Use Plotly?

- Interactive capabilities: Hover effects, zooming, and filtering.
- Supports various chart types, including 3D and geographic plots.
- Works seamlessly in Jupyter Notebooks and web applications.

8.2 Installing Plotly

- Installation command:

bash

pip install plotly

8.3 Using Plotly in Jupyter Notebooks

- To enable interactive output in notebooks:

python

from plotly.offline import init_notebook_mode
init_notebook_mode(connected=True)

Section 2: Creating Basic Interactive Plots

8.4 Line Charts

- Interactive line charts for trends over time.
- **Code Example**:

python

```
import plotly.graph_objects as go

fig = go.Figure()
fig.add_trace(go.Scatter(x=["Jan", "Feb", "Mar"], y=[100, 150, 200],
mode='lines+markers', name="Sales"))
fig.update_layout(title="Interactive Line Chart", xaxis_title="Month",
yaxis_title="Sales")
fig.show()
```

8.5 Bar Charts

- Interactive bar charts for comparing categories.
- **Code Example**:

python

```
fig = go.Figure(data=[go.Bar(x=["A", "B", "C"], y=[10, 20, 15])])
fig.update_layout(title="Interactive           Bar           Chart",
xaxis_title="Categories", yaxis_title="Values")
fig.show()
```

8.6 Scatter Plots

- Visualize relationships with hover effects.
- **Code Example**:

python

```
fig = go.Figure(data=[go.Scatter(x=[1, 2, 3], y=[4, 5, 6],
mode='markers', text=["Point 1", "Point 2", "Point 3"])])
fig.update_layout(title="Interactive Scatter Plot", xaxis_title="X-axis",
yaxis_title="Y-axis")
fig.show()
```

Section 3: Advanced Interactive Features

8.7 Adding Tooltips and Annotations

- Customize hover text and add annotations to highlight key data points.
- **Code Example**:

python

```
fig = go.Figure(data=[go.Scatter(x=[1, 2, 3], y=[4, 5, 6],
mode='markers', text=["Label A", "Label B", "Label C"])])
fig.update_layout(title="Plot with Tooltips", xaxis_title="X-axis",
yaxis_title="Y-axis", annotations=[
    dict(x=2, y=5, text="Important Point", arrowhead=2,
showarrow=True)
])
fig.show()
```

8.8 Subplots and Multi-Chart Layouts

- Combine multiple interactive charts into a single view.
- **Code Example**:

python

```
from plotly.subplots import make_subplots

fig = make_subplots(rows=1, cols=2, subplot_titles=("Scatter Plot", "Bar Chart"))
fig.add_trace(go.Scatter(x=[1, 2, 3], y=[4, 5, 6], mode='markers'), row=1, col=1)
fig.add_trace(go.Bar(x=["A", "B", "C"], y=[10, 20, 15]), row=1, col=2)
fig.update_layout(title="Subplots Example")
fig.show()
```

8.9 Dashboards with Plotly Dash

- Combine multiple charts and widgets into interactive dashboards.
- **Code Example**:

python

```
from dash import Dash, html, dcc

app = Dash(__name__)
app.layout = html.Div([
    html.H1("Interactive Dashboard"),
    dcc.Graph(
```

```
    figure=go.Figure(data=[go.Bar(x=["A",  "B",  "C"],  y=[10,  20,
15])])
     )
])
if __name__ == '__main__':
    app.run_server(debug=True)
```

Section 4: Advanced Customizations and 3D Visualizations

8.10 Customizing Themes and Colors

- Adjust the appearance with predefined templates like plotly_dark.
- **Code Example**:

    python

```
fig = go.Figure(data=[go.Bar(x=["A", "B", "C"], y=[10, 20, 15])])
fig.update_layout(template="plotly_dark")
fig.show()
```

8.11 Creating 3D Plots

- Visualize data in three dimensions for better insight.
- **Code Example**:

    python

```
fig = go.Figure(data=[go.Scatter3d(x=[1, 2, 3], y=[4, 5, 6], z=[7, 8, 9],
mode='markers')])
fig.update_layout(title="3D Scatter Plot")
fig.show()
```

Section 5: Case Study – Interactive Data Exploration

8.12 Dataset: Analyzing Sales Data

1. Load a dataset with columns like Month, Region, and Sales.
2. Steps:
   o Create an interactive line chart to show sales trends by month.
   o Use subplots to compare sales across regions.
   o Add tooltips to display details for each data point.

Chapter Summary

- Plotly enables the creation of interactive and dynamic visualizations with minimal effort.
- Common plots include line charts, bar charts, scatter plots, and 3D plots.
- Advanced features like tooltips, subplots, and dashboards enhance user engagement.

Exercise: Create Interactive Visualizations with Plotly

1. Use Plotly to create an interactive scatter plot with hover text.
2. Combine multiple plots into a subplot layout.
3. Experiment with themes and create a 3D scatter plot.
4. Reflect: How does interactivity improve your data exploration?

Chapter 9: Geospatial Data Visualization

Overview

Geospatial data visualization helps represent data tied to specific locations, enabling insights into spatial patterns and relationships. This chapter focuses on creating interactive and visually appealing maps using Python libraries like Folium and Geopandas, empowering readers to visualize geospatial data effectively.

Key Objectives

By the end of this chapter, readers will:

1. Understand the basics of geospatial data and its significance.
2. Learn to create interactive maps using Folium.
3. Explore Geopandas for handling and visualizing geospatial data.

Section 1: Understanding Geospatial Data

9.1 What is Geospatial Data?

- Data with a geographic component tied to coordinates, addresses, or boundaries.

- Common formats: Shapefiles, GeoJSON, and CSV with latitude/longitude fields.

9.2 Real-World Applications of Geospatial Visualization

- **Urban Planning**: Visualizing population density.
- **Environmental Science**: Mapping deforestation.
- **Business Analytics**: Locating high-demand regions for product delivery.

Section 2: Creating Interactive Maps with Folium

9.3 Introduction to Folium

- Folium is a Python library for creating interactive maps.
- Built on top of Leaflet.js, offering seamless integration with Python.

9.4 Installing Folium

- Installation command:

bash

pip install folium

9.5 Creating a Basic Map

- **Code Example**:

python

import folium

# Create a map centered at a specific location
m = folium.Map(location=[37.7749, -122.4194], zoom_start=12)
m

9.6 Adding Markers and Popups

- Markers represent specific points on the map.
- **Code Example**:

python

folium.Marker(
    location=[37.7749, -122.4194],
    popup="San Francisco",
    icon=folium.Icon(color="blue", icon="info-sign")
).add_to(m)
m

9.7 Adding Layers and Choropleth Maps

- **Choropleth Maps**: Visualize data across geographic regions using color intensity.
- **Code Example**:

```python
python

import pandas as pd

# Sample GeoJSON and data
geojson_url      =      "https://raw.githubusercontent.com/python-
visualization/folium/master/examples/data/us-states.json"
data = pd.DataFrame({
    "State": ["California", "Texas", "New York"],
    "Value": [100, 200, 300]
})

folium.Choropleth(
    geo_data=geojson_url,
    data=data,
    columns=["State", "Value"],
    key_on="feature.id",
    fill_color="YlOrRd",
    fill_opacity=0.7,
    line_opacity=0.2
).add_to(m)
m
```

Section 3: Advanced Geospatial Analysis with Geopandas

9.8 Introduction to Geopandas

- Geopandas extends Pandas with support for spatial operations and geometric types.

- Useful for handling Shapefiles, GeoJSON, and other spatial data formats.

9.9 Installing Geopandas

- Installation command:

bash

```
pip install geopandas
```

9.10 Loading and Exploring Geospatial Data

- Load spatial datasets using Geopandas:

python

```
import geopandas as gpd

# Load a shapefile
gdf = gpd.read_file("path_to_shapefile.shp")
print(gdf.head())
```

9.11 Creating Geospatial Plots

- Use plot() to visualize geometries directly.
- **Code Example**:

python

```
gdf.plot(column="population", cmap="YlOrRd", legend=True)
```

```
plt.title("Population Distribution by Region")
plt.show()
```

9.12 Spatial Operations

- Common operations:
    - **Buffer**: Create zones around a point.
    - **Intersection**: Find overlapping areas between geometries.
    - **Code Example**:

    python

    ```
    point = gpd.GeoSeries([gpd.points_from_xy([1], [1])])
    buffer = point.buffer(0.1)
    buffer.plot()
    plt.title("Buffer Zone Example")
    plt.show()
    ```

Section 4: Combining Folium and Geopandas

9.13 Exporting Geopandas Data to Folium

- Convert Geopandas geometries to GeoJSON for Folium visualization.
- **Code Example**:

    python

```
gdf.to_file("output.geojson", driver="GeoJSON")
folium.GeoJson("output.geojson").add_to(m)
m
```

9.14 Case Study: Mapping COVID-19 Data

1. Dataset: Country-level COVID-19 cases with latitude and longitude.
2. Steps:
   - o Load the dataset into a Pandas DataFrame.
   - o Convert it to a GeoDataFrame using Geopandas.
   - o Visualize the data on an interactive map using Folium.

Chapter Summary

- Geospatial visualization is crucial for understanding spatial patterns and relationships.
- Folium enables interactive map creation with markers, layers, and choropleth maps.
- Geopandas is a powerful tool for geospatial data manipulation and analysis.
- Combining Folium and Geopandas unlocks advanced mapping capabilities.

Exercise: Practice Geospatial Visualization

1. Use a dataset with location data (e.g., city population or weather stations).
2. Create a map with markers using Folium.
3. Plot a choropleth map to visualize a numeric variable by region.
4. Perform a spatial operation with Geopandas, such as creating buffer zones or intersections.

Chapter 10: Time Series Visualizations

Overview

Time series visualization is essential for analyzing trends, patterns, and seasonality in data over time. This chapter explores how to effectively visualize time series data using Python libraries such as Matplotlib, Pandas, and Plotly, demonstrating techniques for both static and interactive charts.

Key Objectives

By the end of this chapter, readers will:

1. Understand the importance of time series visualization in data analysis.
2. Learn to create static time series plots using Matplotlib and Pandas.
3. Explore interactive time series visualizations using Plotly.

Section 1: Introduction to Time Series Data

9.1 What is Time Series Data?

- Data points indexed in time order, typically with regular intervals (e.g., daily, monthly).

- Examples:
  - o Stock prices.
  - o Website traffic.
  - o Weather data.

9.2 Key Elements of Time Series Analysis

1. **Trend**: General direction over time (e.g., upward or downward).
2. **Seasonality**: Repeating patterns (e.g., sales peaking during holidays).
3. **Outliers**: Unusual spikes or dips in the data.

Section 2: Visualizing Time Series Data with Matplotlib

9.3 Basic Line Plots

- Line plots are ideal for visualizing time series trends.
- **Code Example**:

```python
python

import matplotlib.pyplot as plt
import pandas as pd

# Sample data
dates = pd.date_range(start="2023-01-01", periods=10)
```

```
values = [10, 15, 20, 25, 30, 35, 40, 45, 50, 55]

plt.plot(dates, values)
plt.title("Time Series Visualization")
plt.xlabel("Date")
plt.ylabel("Value")
plt.grid(True)
plt.show()
```

9.4 Adding Annotations

- Highlight key events on the time series plot.
- **Code Example**:

python

```
plt.plot(dates, values)
plt.title("Time Series with Annotation")
plt.xlabel("Date")
plt.ylabel("Value")
plt.annotate("Peak", xy=(dates[9], values[9]), xytext=(dates[8], values[8] + 10),
        arrowprops=dict(facecolor='red', arrowstyle="->"))
plt.grid(True)
plt.show()
```

9.5 Multiple Time Series on One Plot

- Compare trends across multiple datasets.
- **Code Example**:

```
python

values_2 = [5, 10, 15, 20, 25, 30, 35, 40, 45, 50]

plt.plot(dates, values, label="Series 1")
plt.plot(dates, values_2, label="Series 2", linestyle="--")
plt.title("Comparing Time Series")
plt.xlabel("Date")
plt.ylabel("Value")
plt.legend()
plt.grid(True)
plt.show()
```

Section 3: Leveraging Pandas for Time Series Visualization

9.6 Using Pandas Plotting

- Quickly visualize time series data from a Pandas DataFrame.
- **Code Example**:

```
python

df = pd.DataFrame({"Date": dates, "Value": values})
df.set_index("Date").plot()
plt.title("Time Series Plot with Pandas")
plt.show()
```

9.7 Handling Missing Data

- Fill missing data points to ensure smooth visualizations.
- **Code Example**:

python

```
df.loc[3, "Value"] = None
df["Value"] = df["Value"].interpolate()
df.set_index("Date").plot()
plt.title("Time Series with Missing Data Filled")
plt.show()
```

Section 4: Interactive Time Series with Plotly

9.8 Creating Interactive Line Charts

- Use Plotly for dynamic time series visualizations.
- **Code Example**:

python

```
import plotly.graph_objects as go

fig = go.Figure()
fig.add_trace(go.Scatter(x=dates, y=values, mode='lines+markers', name="Time Series"))
fig.update_layout(title="Interactive Time Series", xaxis_title="Date", yaxis_title="Value")
fig.show()
```

9.9 Adding Ranges and Sliders

- Allow users to zoom and filter data interactively.
- **Code Example**:

python

```
fig.update_layout(
    xaxis=dict(
        rangeslider=dict(visible=True),
        rangeselector=dict(
            buttons=[
                dict(count=1,        label="1m",        step="month",
stepmode="backward"),
                dict(count=6,        label="6m",        step="month",
stepmode="backward"),
                dict(step="all")
            ]
        )
    )
)
fig.show()
```

Section 5: Advanced Time Series Visualizations

9.10 Highlighting Trends and Seasonality

- Decompose time series to analyze components like trends and seasonality.

- **Code Example**:

python

```
from statsmodels.tsa.seasonal import seasonal_decompose

series = pd.Series(values, index=dates)
decomposition = seasonal_decompose(series, model='additive', period=3)
decomposition.plot()
plt.show()
```

9.11 Time Series Heatmaps

- Visualize data intensity across time intervals.
- **Code Example**:

python

```
import seaborn as sns
import numpy as np

heatmap_data = np.random.rand(10, 12)
sns.heatmap(heatmap_data, cmap="YlGnBu", xticklabels=["Jan", "Feb", "Mar", "Apr", "May", "Jun", "Jul", "Aug", "Sep", "Oct", "Nov", "Dec"])
plt.title("Time Series Heatmap")
plt.show()
```

Section 6: Case Study – Analyzing Stock Prices

9.12 Dataset: Daily Stock Prices

1. Load a dataset with columns like Date, Open, Close, and Volume.
2. Steps:
   - Plot daily closing prices using Matplotlib.
   - Use Plotly to create an interactive chart with volume bars.
   - Highlight trends using decomposition.

Chapter Summary

- Time series visualizations reveal trends, seasonality, and anomalies in data over time.
- Matplotlib and Pandas offer robust static visualizations.
- Plotly provides dynamic, interactive charts ideal for exploratory analysis.

Exercise: Visualize a Time Series Dataset

1. Load a time series dataset (e.g., weather, stock prices, or sales).

2. Create a static visualization using Matplotlib or Pandas.

3. Build an interactive time series plot with Plotly, adding zoom and range selectors.

4. Decompose the time series to analyze trends and seasonality.

Chapter 11: Visualizing Networks and Graphs

Overview

Networks and graphs are crucial for representing relationships between entities, such as social networks, transportation routes, or web connections. This chapter explores how to visualize and analyze network data using the NetworkX library in Python, emphasizing clarity, aesthetics, and insights.

Key Objectives

By the end of this chapter, readers will:

1. Understand the fundamentals of network and graph data.
2. Learn to create and visualize graphs using NetworkX.
3. Explore advanced techniques for analyzing and styling network visualizations.

Section 1: Understanding Networks and Graphs

10.1 What Are Networks and Graphs?

- A **graph** is a collection of nodes (or vertices) connected by edges.
  - **Nodes**: Represent entities (e.g., people, cities, or devices).
  - **Edges**: Represent relationships or connections (e.g., friendships, routes).
- Types of Graphs:
  - **Undirected**: Edges have no direction (e.g., mutual friendships).
  - **Directed**: Edges have a direction (e.g., follower relationships on Twitter).
  - **Weighted**: Edges have weights (e.g., distances, costs).

10.2 Real-World Applications

1. **Social Networks**: Understanding relationships and influence.
2. **Transportation**: Visualizing routes and optimizing paths.
3. **Web Analytics**: Representing website connections and user behavior.

Section 2: Introduction to NetworkX

10.3 Why Use NetworkX?

- Simplifies the creation, manipulation, and visualization of network data.
- Provides tools for analyzing graph properties like centrality and shortest paths.

10.4 Installing NetworkX

- Installation command:

bash

pip install networkx

Section 3: Creating and Visualizing Graphs

10.5 Building a Basic Graph

- **Code Example**:

python

```
import networkx as nx
import matplotlib.pyplot as plt

# Create a graph
G = nx.Graph()
G.add_nodes_from(["A", "B", "C", "D"])
G.add_edges_from([("A", "B"), ("B", "C"), ("C", "D"), ("D", "A")])
```

```python
# Visualize the graph
nx.draw(G, with_labels=True, node_color="lightblue",
edge_color="gray")
plt.title("Basic Graph Visualization")
plt.show()
```

10.6 Directed Graphs

- Represent connections with directionality.
- **Code Example**:

python

```python
DG = nx.DiGraph()
DG.add_edges_from([("A", "B"), ("B", "C"), ("C", "A")])

nx.draw(DG, with_labels=True, node_color="lightgreen",
edge_color="black", arrowsize=20)
plt.title("Directed Graph")
plt.show()
```

10.7 Weighted Graphs

- Include weights for edges to represent strengths or costs.
- **Code Example**:

python

```python
WG = nx.Graph()
WG.add_edge("A", "B", weight=4)
WG.add_edge("B", "C", weight=7)
```

```
pos = nx.spring_layout(WG)
nx.draw(WG, pos, with_labels=True, node_color="orange")
labels = nx.get_edge_attributes(WG, "weight")
nx.draw_networkx_edge_labels(WG, pos, edge_labels=labels)
plt.title("Weighted Graph")
plt.show()
```

Section 4: Analyzing Networks

10.8 Calculating Graph Properties

1. **Degree Centrality**: Measure of node connectivity.
2. **Shortest Paths**: Minimum steps between nodes.

- **Code Example**:

python

```
print("Degree Centrality:", nx.degree_centrality(G))
print("Shortest Path from A to D:", nx.shortest_path(G, source="A",
target="D"))
```

10.9 Communities in Networks

- Detect clusters of tightly connected nodes.
- **Code Example**:

python

```
from          networkx.algorithms.community          import
greedy_modularity_communities

communities = list(greedy_modularity_communities(G))
print("Communities:", communities)
```

Section 5: Advanced Network Visualization

10.10 Styling Graph Visualizations

- Customize node sizes, edge colors, and labels.
- **Code Example**:

python

```
nx.draw(
    G,
    with_labels=True,
    node_size=[300 * G.degree(n) for n in G.nodes],
    node_color="skyblue",
    edge_color="black",
    font_size=10
)
plt.title("Styled Network Visualization")
plt.show()
```

10.11 Interactive Graph Visualizations with Plotly

- Combine NetworkX and Plotly for interactive exploration.
- **Code Example**:

python

```
import plotly.graph_objects as go

pos = nx.spring_layout(G)
edge_x = []
edge_y = []
for edge in G.edges():
    x0, y0 = pos[edge[0]]
    x1, y1 = pos[edge[1]]
    edge_x.append(x0)
    edge_x.append(x1)
    edge_x.append(None)
    edge_y.append(y0)
    edge_y.append(y1)
    edge_y.append(None)

edge_trace = go.Scatter(x=edge_x, y=edge_y, line=dict(width=0.5,
color="gray"), hoverinfo="none", mode="lines")

node_x = []
node_y = []
for node in G.nodes():
    x, y = pos[node]
    node_x.append(x)
    node_y.append(y)
```

```
node_trace = go.Scatter(x=node_x, y=node_y, mode="markers+text",
text=list(G.nodes()),
            marker=dict(size=10, color="blue"))

fig = go.Figure(data=[edge_trace, node_trace])
fig.update_layout(title="Interactive    Network    Visualization",
showlegend=False)
fig.show()
```

Section 6: Case Study – Social Network Analysis

10.12 Dataset: Social Media Interactions

1. Load a dataset representing interactions (e.g., followers, likes, or messages).

2. Steps:

    o Create a directed graph to represent follower relationships.

    o Calculate centrality measures to identify influential users.

    o Visualize the network with node sizes based on centrality.

Chapter Summary

- Networks and graphs are essential for representing relationships in various domains.
- NetworkX provides robust tools for creating, analyzing, and visualizing network data.
- Advanced visualizations and analysis reveal meaningful insights into network structure.

Exercise: Practice Network Visualization

1. Create a graph to represent a small network (e.g., transportation routes, friendships).
2. Add weights or directions to edges and visualize the graph.
3. Analyze graph properties like centrality or shortest paths.
4. Create an interactive visualization using Plotly.

Chapter 12: Customizing Visualizations for Storytelling

Overview

Effective storytelling with data requires more than just presenting numbers—it involves crafting visualizations that resonate with the audience, highlight key insights, and guide interpretation. This chapter focuses on customizing visualizations to create compelling narratives, combining design principles with data storytelling techniques.

Key Objectives

By the end of this chapter, readers will:

1. Understand the principles of storytelling in data visualization.
2. Learn to customize visual elements to emphasize key insights.
3. Use annotations, colors, and layout techniques to craft narratives.

Section 1: The Principles of Storytelling with Data

12.1 Why Storytelling Matters in Visualization

- Data storytelling transforms raw numbers into actionable insights.
- Combines visuals, context, and narrative to communicate effectively.

12.2 Key Components of Data Storytelling

1. **Audience**: Tailor visuals to the knowledge and needs of your viewers.
2. **Focus**: Highlight the most important insights to avoid overwhelming the audience.
3. **Flow**: Guide the viewer through the story with logical progression and design.

Section 2: Enhancing Visuals for Storytelling

12.3 Using Annotations for Clarity

- Add context to specific points or trends with annotations.
- **Code Example (Matplotlib)**:

python

```
import matplotlib.pyplot as plt
```

```python
x = [1, 2, 3, 4, 5]
y = [10, 20, 15, 25, 30]

plt.plot(x, y)
plt.title("Annotated Line Chart")
plt.xlabel("Time")
plt.ylabel("Value")
plt.annotate("Significant Increase", xy=(4, 25), xytext=(3, 20),
        arrowprops=dict(facecolor="red", arrowstyle="->"))
plt.show()
```

12.4 Choosing the Right Colors

- Use color to highlight key data points or categories.
  - **Consistent Palettes**: Maintain brand identity or thematic consistency.
  - **Contrast**: Use contrasting colors to draw attention.
- **Code Example (Seaborn)**:

python

```python
import seaborn as sns
import pandas as pd

data = {"Category": ["A", "B", "C"], "Values": [30, 70, 50]}
df = pd.DataFrame(data)

sns.barplot(x="Category", y="Values", data=df, palette="coolwarm")
plt.title("Custom Color Palette Example")
```

```
plt.show()
```

12.5 Highlighting Key Data Points

- Emphasize critical insights with custom markers or labels.
- **Code Example (Matplotlib)**:

python

```
plt.plot(x, y, marker="o", markersize=8, markerfacecolor="red")
plt.title("Highlighted Data Points")
plt.show()
```

Section 3: Structuring Visualizations for Narrative Flow

12.6 Guiding Attention with Layouts

- Use whitespace and alignment to direct focus.
- Arrange multiple charts to support the narrative.
- **Code Example (Matplotlib Subplots)**:

python

```
fig, axs = plt.subplots(2, 1, figsize=(8, 10))
axs[0].plot(x, y, label="Trend 1", color="blue")
axs[0].set_title("Overall Trend")
axs[1].bar(["A", "B", "C"], [10, 20, 15], color="green")
axs[1].set_title("Category Breakdown")
plt.tight_layout()
```

```
plt.show()
```

12.7 Adding Context with Supporting Text

- Use subtitles, captions, and legends to provide additional information.
- **Code Example (Matplotlib)**:

python

```
plt.plot(x, y)
plt.title("Revenue Growth Over Time", fontsize=14)
plt.suptitle("Analyzing Quarterly Trends (2023)", fontsize=10,
color="gray")
plt.xlabel("Quarter")
plt.ylabel("Revenue")
plt.legend(["Growth Rate"], loc="upper left")
plt.show()
```

Section 4: Tools for Interactive Storytelling

12.8 Interactivity with Plotly

- Allow users to explore data by hovering, zooming, and filtering.
- **Code Example**:

python

```
import plotly.graph_objects as go

fig = go.Figure(data=go.Scatter(x=x, y=y, mode="lines+markers",
text=["Q1", "Q2", "Q3", "Q4", "Q5"]))
fig.update_layout(title="Interactive     Storytelling     with     Plotly",
xaxis_title="Quarter", yaxis_title="Revenue")
fig.show()
```

12.9 Dashboards for Narrative Flow

- Combine multiple visualizations in dashboards using Plotly Dash or Tableau.
- **Code Example (Plotly Dash)**:

python

```
from dash import Dash, html, dcc

app = Dash(__name__)
app.layout = html.Div([
    html.H1("Revenue Dashboard"),
    dcc.Graph(
        figure=go.Figure(data=go.Scatter(x=x, y=y, mode="lines"))
    ),
    dcc.Graph(
        figure=go.Figure(data=go.Bar(x=["A", "B", "C"], y=[10, 20, 15]))
    )
])
if __name__ == "__main__":
    app.run_server(debug=True)
```

Section 5: Case Study – Telling a Sales Growth Story

12.10 Dataset: Quarterly Sales and Expenses

1. Load a dataset with Quarter, Sales, and Expenses.
2. Steps:
   - Highlight the quarter with the highest growth.
   - Use annotations to explain sudden dips or spikes.
   - Create a dashboard combining sales trends and expense breakdowns.

Chapter Summary

- Storytelling with visualizations enhances communication and audience engagement.
- Annotations, colors, and layouts guide viewers through the narrative.
- Interactive tools like Plotly and dashboards enable deeper exploration of the story.

Exercise: Create a Storytelling Visualization

1. Use a dataset with time series or categorical data.

2. Design a visualization with annotations and customized colors.

3. Build a dashboard or interactive chart to complement the story.

4. Reflect: How does the design enhance the story you want to tell?

Chapter 13: Dashboards with Dash and Streamlit

Overview

Dashboards are powerful tools for aggregating and displaying key metrics and insights in an interactive, user-friendly format. This chapter explores building dashboards with two popular Python frameworks: Dash and Streamlit. You'll learn how to create engaging dashboards that allow users to explore and interact with data.

Key Objectives

By the end of this chapter, readers will:

1. Understand the purpose and components of dashboards.
2. Learn to build interactive dashboards with Dash.
3. Explore rapid dashboard development using Streamlit.

Section 1: Introduction to Dashboards

13.1 What is a Dashboard?

- A dashboard is an interface that displays data visualizations, metrics, and interactive elements.
- Key characteristics:
    o **Interactive**: Users can filter and explore data.
    o **Informative**: Displays key metrics at a glance.
    o **User-Friendly**: Intuitive design for seamless exploration.

13.2 Applications of Dashboards

- **Business**: Sales performance, financial metrics.
- **Healthcare**: Patient monitoring, outbreak tracking.
- **Marketing**: Campaign performance, audience insights.

Section 2: Building Dashboards with Dash

13.3 Introduction to Dash

- A Python framework for building interactive web applications and dashboards.
- Built on top of Flask, Plotly, and React.js.

13.4 Installing Dash

- Installation command:

bash

pip install dash

13.5 Creating a Simple Dashboard

- **Code Example**:

python

```python
from dash import Dash, html, dcc
import plotly.express as px
import pandas as pd

# Sample data
df = pd.DataFrame({
    "Fruit": ["Apples", "Oranges", "Bananas", "Grapes"],
    "Sales": [120, 200, 150, 90]
})

# Create app
app = Dash(__name__)
fig = px.bar(df, x="Fruit", y="Sales", title="Fruit Sales")

app.layout = html.Div([
    html.H1("Sales Dashboard"),
    dcc.Graph(figure=fig)
])

if __name__ == "__main__":
    app.run_server(debug=True)
```

13.6 Adding Interactivity

- Use dcc.Dropdown for filtering data.
- **Code Example**:

python

```python
from dash.dependencies import Input, Output

app.layout = html.Div([
    html.H1("Interactive Sales Dashboard"),
    dcc.Dropdown(
        id="fruit-dropdown",
        options=[{"label": fruit, "value": fruit} for fruit in df["Fruit"]],
        value="Apples"
    ),
    dcc.Graph(id="sales-bar")
])

@app.callback(
    Output("sales-bar", "figure"),
    [Input("fruit-dropdown", "value")]
)
def update_chart(selected_fruit):
    filtered_df = df[df["Fruit"] == selected_fruit]
    fig = px.bar(filtered_df, x="Fruit", y="Sales")
    return fig

if __name__ == "__main__":
    app.run_server(debug=True)
```

Section 3: Building Dashboards with Streamlit

13.7 Introduction to Streamlit

- A Python library for quickly creating interactive web applications with minimal code.
- Focuses on simplicity and rapid prototyping.

13.8 Installing Streamlit

- Installation command:

  bash

  pip install streamlit

13.9 Creating a Simple Dashboard

- **Code Example**:

  python

  ```python
  import streamlit as st
  import pandas as pd
  import plotly.express as px

  # Sample data
  df = pd.DataFrame({
  ```

```
"Fruit": ["Apples", "Oranges", "Bananas", "Grapes"],
"Sales": [120, 200, 150, 90]
})
```

```
st.title("Sales Dashboard")
st.plotly_chart(px.bar(df, x="Fruit", y="Sales", title="Fruit Sales"))
```

- Run the app with:

bash

streamlit run app.py

13.10 Adding Interactivity

- Use widgets like st.selectbox for user input.
- **Code Example**:

python

```
selected_fruit = st.selectbox("Select a fruit:", df["Fruit"])
filtered_df = df[df["Fruit"] == selected_fruit]
st.write(f"Sales for {selected_fruit}: {filtered_df['Sales'].values[0]}")
st.plotly_chart(px.bar(filtered_df, x="Fruit", y="Sales", title=f"Sales for {selected_fruit}"))
```

Section 4: Comparing Dash and Streamlit

Feature	Dash	Streamlit
Complexity	Requires callbacks and structure	Minimal code, rapid setup
Customization	Highly customizable	Limited compared to Dash
Use Case	Production-level apps	Prototypes and quick demos

Section 5: Case Study – Creating a Sales Dashboard

13.11 Dataset: Monthly Sales Data

1. **Dash Implementation**:
   o Include a line chart for monthly trends.
   o Add dropdowns for region selection.
2. **Streamlit Implementation**:
   o Create a sidebar for user inputs.
   o Use widgets to toggle between sales and profit visualizations.

Chapter Summary

- Dash and Streamlit simplify the creation of user-friendly dashboards.
- Dash is ideal for complex, production-level applications with advanced interactivity.
- Streamlit excels at rapid prototyping with minimal setup.

Exercise: Build Your Own Dashboard

1. Use a dataset with multiple metrics (e.g., sales, profit, and region).
2. Create an interactive dashboard using Dash or Streamlit.
3. Add filters, charts, and key metrics for user exploration.
4. Reflect: Which framework felt more intuitive for your use case?

Chapter 14: 3D Visualizations

Overview

3D visualizations add a new dimension to data representation, allowing viewers to explore complex relationships in spatial or multi-dimensional datasets. This chapter covers the creation of 3D visualizations using Plotly and Matplotlib, focusing on their applications, techniques, and customization.

Key Objectives

By the end of this chapter, readers will:

1. Understand the importance of 3D visualizations in data analysis.
2. Create and customize 3D plots using Plotly.
3. Explore Matplotlib's 3D capabilities for static and interactive visualizations.

Section 1: Introduction to 3D Visualizations

14.1 Why Use 3D Visualizations?

- Useful for visualizing data with three or more variables.

- Enables spatial analysis (e.g., geographic data, scientific simulations).
- Adds depth to scatter plots, surface plots, and bar charts.

14.2 Applications of 3D Visualization

- **Scientific Research**: Representing molecular structures or simulations.
- **Business Analytics**: Visualizing sales across regions and time.
- **Engineering**: Simulating designs or processes.

Section 2: 3D Visualization with Plotly

14.3 Introduction to Plotly's 3D Capabilities

- Plotly provides intuitive and interactive 3D visualizations.
- Popular 3D plot types: scatter, surface, and mesh grids.

14.4 Creating a 3D Scatter Plot

- **Code Example**:

python

```
import plotly.graph_objects as go
```

```python
x = [1, 2, 3, 4, 5]
y = [10, 20, 30, 40, 50]
z = [100, 200, 300, 400, 500]

fig = go.Figure(data=[go.Scatter3d(x=x, y=y, z=z, mode='markers', marker=dict(size=5, color=z, colorscale='Viridis'))])
fig.update_layout(title="3D Scatter Plot", scene=dict(xaxis_title="X", yaxis_title="Y", zaxis_title="Z"))
fig.show()
```

14.5 Creating a 3D Surface Plot

- Ideal for visualizing data across two continuous variables.
- **Code Example**:

```python
python

import numpy as np

x = np.linspace(-5, 5, 100)
y = np.linspace(-5, 5, 100)
X, Y = np.meshgrid(x, y)
Z = np.sin(np.sqrt(X**2 + Y**2))

fig = go.Figure(data=[go.Surface(z=Z, x=X, y=Y)])
fig.update_layout(title="3D Surface Plot", scene=dict(xaxis_title="X", yaxis_title="Y", zaxis_title="Z"))
fig.show()
```

14.6 Customizing 3D Plots

- Add annotations and adjust the view angle:

python

```
fig.update_layout(scene_camera=dict(eye=dict(x=1.5, y=1.5, z=1.5)))
fig.show()
```

Section 3: 3D Visualization with Matplotlib

14.7 Introduction to Matplotlib's 3D Toolkit

- Matplotlib supports 3D plotting through the mpl_toolkits.mplot3d module.

14.8 Creating a 3D Scatter Plot

- **Code Example**:

python

```
import matplotlib.pyplot as plt
from mpl_toolkits.mplot3d import Axes3D

fig = plt.figure()
ax = fig.add_subplot(111, projection='3d')

x = [1, 2, 3, 4, 5]
y = [10, 20, 30, 40, 50]
z = [100, 200, 300, 400, 500]
```

```
ax.scatter(x, y, z, c='r', marker='o')
ax.set_title("3D Scatter Plot")
ax.set_xlabel("X")
ax.set_ylabel("Y")
ax.set_zlabel("Z")

plt.show()
```

14.9 Creating a 3D Surface Plot

- **Code Example**:

```
python

import numpy as np

fig = plt.figure()
ax = fig.add_subplot(111, projection='3d')

x = np.linspace(-5, 5, 100)
y = np.linspace(-5, 5, 100)
X, Y = np.meshgrid(x, y)
Z = np.sin(np.sqrt(X**2 + Y**2))

ax.plot_surface(X, Y, Z, cmap='viridis')
ax.set_title("3D Surface Plot")
ax.set_xlabel("X")
ax.set_ylabel("Y")
ax.set_zlabel("Z")
```

```
plt.show()
```

14.10 Customizing Matplotlib 3D Plots

- Adjust viewpoints, color maps, and add contour projections:

python

```
ax.view_init(elev=30, azim=45)
plt.show()
```

Section 4: Comparing Plotly and Matplotlib for 3D Visualization

Feature	Plotly	Matplotlib
Interactivity	Highly interactive	Limited interactivity
Ease of Use	Intuitive for 3D plots	Requires more configuration
Customization	Advanced, dynamic styling	Static, traditional styling
Best For	Exploratory analysis	Publication-quality plots

Section 5: Case Study – Visualizing Geographic Data in 3D

14.11 Dataset: Elevation Data of a Region

1. Load elevation data for a geographic region.
2. Steps:
    - ○ Create a 3D surface plot to represent the elevation.
    - ○ Customize colors to reflect different elevation ranges.
    - ○ Use Plotly for an interactive exploration of the terrain.

Chapter Summary

- 3D visualizations provide insights into multi-dimensional datasets.
- Plotly excels in interactive and dynamic 3D plotting.
- Matplotlib is well-suited for static, publication-ready 3D plots.

Exercise: Practice 3D Visualization

1. Create a 3D scatter plot for a dataset with three numerical columns.
2. Visualize a mathematical function (e.g., sine waves) as a 3D surface plot.
3. Use Plotly to add interactivity, such as zooming and rotating.

4. Reflect: Which library felt more intuitive for your needs, and why?

Chapter 15: Data Animation for Dynamic Visuals

Overview

Animations in data visualization add a dynamic element, helping users observe changes over time or across variables. This chapter covers creating animations using Python libraries like Matplotlib and Plotly, highlighting techniques for making data animations engaging and effective.

Key Objectives

By the end of this chapter, readers will:

1. Understand the role of animations in data visualization.
2. Create animations with Matplotlib for static and interactive outputs.
3. Explore Plotly's capabilities for smooth, interactive animations.

Section 1: The Importance of Data Animation

15.1 Why Animate Data?

- Visualizing trends, patterns, or changes dynamically.
- Engaging and intuitive way to present complex data.
- Examples:
  - Tracking stock market trends over time.
  - Showing the spread of a phenomenon (e.g., COVID-19 cases).

15.2 Real-World Applications

1. **Finance**: Visualizing stock movements.
2. **Environment**: Animating temperature changes over decades.
3. **Marketing**: Tracking customer engagement trends.

Section 2: Animations with Matplotlib

15.3 Setting Up Matplotlib for Animations

- Use matplotlib.animation for creating animations.
- Install FFMpeg or ImageMagick for saving animations as videos or GIFs.

15.4 Creating a Basic Animation

- **Code Example:**

python

```python
import matplotlib.pyplot as plt
from matplotlib.animation import FuncAnimation
import numpy as np

fig, ax = plt.subplots()
x = np.linspace(0, 2 * np.pi, 100)
y = np.sin(x)
line, = ax.plot(x, y)

def update(frame):
    line.set_ydata(np.sin(x + frame / 10))
    return line,

ani = FuncAnimation(fig, update, frames=100, interval=50)
plt.show()
```

15.5 Saving the Animation

- Save the animation as a video or GIF:

python

```python
ani.save("sine_wave_animation.mp4", writer="ffmpeg")
```

15.6 Animated Scatter Plots

- Show dynamic changes in scatter plot data.
- **Code Example**:

```python
python

fig, ax = plt.subplots()
scatter = ax.scatter([], [], s=50)

def init():
    ax.set_xlim(0, 10)
    ax.set_ylim(0, 10)
    return scatter,

def update(frame):
    x = np.random.rand(10) * 10
    y = np.random.rand(10) * 10
    scatter.set_offsets(np.c_[x, y])
    return scatter,

ani = FuncAnimation(fig, update, frames=50, init_func=init, blit=True)
plt.show()
```

Section 3: Animations with Plotly

15.7 Introduction to Plotly Animations

- Plotly simplifies animation creation with built-in support for animated frames.
- Ideal for interactive, browser-based visualizations.

15.8 Creating an Animated Scatter Plot

- **Code Example**:

python

```python
import plotly.express as px
import pandas as pd

df = pd.DataFrame({
    "x": [1, 2, 3, 4, 5, 1, 2, 3, 4, 5],
    "y": [1, 4, 9, 16, 25, 2, 5, 10, 17, 26],
    "frame": [1, 1, 1, 1, 1, 2, 2, 2, 2, 2]
})

fig = px.scatter(df, x="x", y="y", animation_frame="frame",
title="Animated Scatter Plot")
fig.show()
```

15.9 Animated Line Charts

- Show trends evolving over time.
- **Code Example**:

python

```python
df = pd.DataFrame({
    "x": [1, 2, 3, 4, 5] * 2,
    "y": [1, 2, 4, 8, 16, 1, 3, 6, 9, 12],
    "frame": [1, 1, 1, 1, 1, 2, 2, 2, 2, 2]
})
```

```
fig    =    px.line(df,    x="x",    y="y",    animation_frame="frame",
title="Animated Line Chart")
fig.show()
```

Section 4: Advanced Animation Techniques

15.10 Customizing Animation Timing

- Adjust frame duration and easing for smoother transitions.
- **Code Example (Plotly):**

python

```
fig.update_layout(updatemenus=[{
    "buttons": [
        {"label": "Play", "method": "animate", "args": [None, {"frame":
{"duration": 500, "redraw": True}}]},
        {"label": "Pause", "method": "animate", "args": [[None], {"frame":
{"duration": 0, "redraw": False}}]}
    ]
}])
fig.show()
```

15.11 Combining Animations with Annotations

- Highlight trends or anomalies dynamically.
- **Code Example (Matplotlib):**

python

```
def update(frame):
    line.set_ydata(np.sin(x + frame / 10))
    ax.annotate(f"Frame: {frame}", xy=(0.8, 0.9), xycoords="axes
fraction")
    return line,

ani = FuncAnimation(fig, update, frames=100, interval=50)
plt.show()
```

Section 5: Case Study – Animating Population Growth Over Time

15.12 Dataset: Population Data by Year

1. Load a dataset with population changes over decades.
2. Steps:

    o Use Matplotlib to create a line chart animation showing global population growth.

    o Create a Plotly animation comparing population trends across countries.

Chapter Summary

- Animations make data visualization dynamic, intuitive, and engaging.
- Matplotlib is excellent for basic, programmatic animations.
- Plotly simplifies creating interactive animations ideal for web applications.

Exercise: Create an Animated Visualization

1. Use a dataset with a time dimension (e.g., sales over months, stock prices).
2. Create an animated line chart with Matplotlib.
3. Build an interactive animated scatter plot with Plotly.
4. Reflect: How does animation enhance the story your data tells?

Chapter 16: Integrating Machine Learning Results into Visuals

Overview

Machine learning models generate valuable insights, but their results often need to be visualized effectively to make them understandable and actionable. This chapter covers techniques for visualizing machine learning results, including model performance metrics, predictions, and feature importance, using libraries like Matplotlib, Seaborn, and Plotly.

Key Objectives

By the end of this chapter, readers will:

1. Understand the importance of visualizing machine learning results.
2. Learn to visualize model performance, predictions, and feature importance.
3. Use Python libraries to create clear and engaging visualizations for ML insights.

Section 1: Importance of Visualizing ML Results

16.1 Why Visualize ML Results?

- Make complex models understandable to non-technical stakeholders.
- Evaluate model performance and identify areas for improvement.
- Communicate key insights, such as influential features and predictions.

16.2 Common ML Visualization Needs

1. **Performance Metrics**: Accuracy, precision, recall, F1-score.
2. **Predictions**: Comparison of predicted vs. actual values.
3. **Feature Importance**: Identifying key drivers of the model.

Section 2: Visualizing Model Performance

16.3 Confusion Matrix

- Visualize classification performance.
- **Code Example (Seaborn)**:

python

```
from sklearn.metrics import confusion_matrix, ConfusionMatrixDisplay
```

```
import seaborn as sns
import matplotlib.pyplot as plt


y_true = [0, 1, 1, 0, 1]
y_pred = [0, 1, 1, 0, 0]
cm = confusion_matrix(y_true, y_pred)


sns.heatmap(cm, annot=True, fmt="d", cmap="Blues")
plt.title("Confusion Matrix")
plt.xlabel("Predicted")
plt.ylabel("Actual")
plt.show()
```

16.4 ROC Curve

- Evaluate classifier performance across thresholds.
- **Code Example (Matplotlib):**

python

```
from sklearn.metrics import roc_curve, auc
import numpy as np


y_scores = np.array([0.1, 0.4, 0.35, 0.8, 0.6])
y_true = np.array([0, 0, 1, 1, 1])
fpr, tpr, _ = roc_curve(y_true, y_scores)
roc_auc = auc(fpr, tpr)


plt.plot(fpr, tpr, label=f"AUC = {roc_auc:.2f}")
plt.title("ROC Curve")
```

```
plt.xlabel("False Positive Rate")
plt.ylabel("True Positive Rate")
plt.legend(loc="lower right")
plt.show()
```

Section 3: Visualizing Predictions

16.5 Actual vs. Predicted Values

- Compare predicted outcomes with actual data.
- **Code Example (Seaborn)**:

  python

  ```
  import pandas as pd
  import seaborn as sns

  df = pd.DataFrame({"Actual": [10, 20, 30, 40, 50], "Predicted": [12, 22, 29, 38, 48]})
  sns.scatterplot(x="Actual", y="Predicted", data=df)
  plt.plot([0, 60], [0, 60], linestyle="--", color="red")  # Reference line
  plt.title("Actual vs. Predicted")
  plt.xlabel("Actual")
  plt.ylabel("Predicted")
  plt.show()
  ```

16.6 Residual Plots

- Identify patterns in prediction errors.

- **Code Example (Matplotlib)**:

python

```
residuals = df["Actual"] - df["Predicted"]
plt.scatter(df["Predicted"], residuals)
plt.axhline(0, color="red", linestyle="--")
plt.title("Residual Plot")
plt.xlabel("Predicted")
plt.ylabel("Residuals")
plt.show()
```

Section 4: Visualizing Feature Importance

16.7 Bar Plot for Feature Importance

- Show how much each feature contributes to predictions.
- **Code Example (Seaborn)**:

python

```
feature_importance = {"Feature": ["A", "B", "C", "D"], "Importance": [0.4, 0.3, 0.2, 0.1]}
df = pd.DataFrame(feature_importance)

sns.barplot(x="Importance", y="Feature", data=df, palette="viridis")
plt.title("Feature Importance")
plt.show()
```

16.8 SHAP Values

- Use SHAP (SHapley Additive exPlanations) for detailed feature importance.
- **Code Example**:

python

```python
import shap
import xgboost as xgb

# Example with XGBoost model
model = xgb.XGBRegressor()
X_train = pd.DataFrame({"A": [1, 2, 3], "B": [4, 5, 6], "C": [7, 8, 9]})
y_train = [10, 20, 30]
model.fit(X_train, y_train)

explainer = shap.Explainer(model)
shap_values = explainer(X_train)

shap.summary_plot(shap_values, X_train)
```

Section 5: Interactive ML Visualizations with Plotly

16.9 Feature Importance Plot

- Make feature importance interactive.
- **Code Example (Plotly)**:

python

```
import plotly.express as px

df = pd.DataFrame({"Feature": ["A", "B", "C", "D"], "Importance": [0.4,
0.3, 0.2, 0.1]})
fig = px.bar(df, x="Importance", y="Feature", orientation="h",
title="Interactive Feature Importance")
fig.show()
```

16.10 Predictions Over Time

- Visualize predictions and actual values dynamically.
- **Code Example (Plotly)**:

python

```
df = pd.DataFrame({"Time": [1, 2, 3, 4, 5], "Actual": [10, 20, 30, 40,
50], "Predicted": [12, 22, 29, 38, 48]})
fig = px.line(df, x="Time", y=["Actual", "Predicted"], title="Predictions
Over Time")
fig.show()
```

Section 6: Case Study – Visualizing ML Results for a Sales Prediction Model

16.11 Dataset: Predicting Monthly Sales

1. **Performance Metrics**:

      ○ Use confusion matrices and ROC curves to evaluate the model.

2. **Predictions**:

      ○ Plot actual vs. predicted sales.

3. **Feature Importance**:

      ○ Visualize the top drivers of sales predictions.

Chapter Summary

- Visualizing machine learning results makes complex models interpretable.
- Use confusion matrices, ROC curves, and feature importance charts to communicate performance and insights.
- Combine static and interactive plots for engaging presentations.

Exercise: Create ML Visualizations

1. Train a machine learning model on a dataset (e.g., house prices, sales, or customer churn).
2. Visualize performance metrics like confusion matrix or ROC curve.
3. Plot actual vs. predicted values and feature importance.

4. Reflect: How do these visualizations enhance model understanding and communication?

Chapter 17: Business Data Visualization

Overview

Data visualization is critical for making informed business decisions. This chapter explores how to create effective visuals for sales, marketing, and finance insights using Python libraries like Matplotlib, Seaborn, and Plotly. These visuals will help businesses identify trends, optimize performance, and communicate results effectively.

Key Objectives

By the end of this chapter, readers will:

1. Understand the importance of data visualization in business.
2. Learn to create visuals for sales, marketing, and financial insights.
3. Use Python libraries to create actionable and engaging business-focused charts.

Section 1: The Importance of Visualization in Business

17.1 Why Visualize Business Data?

- Simplifies complex datasets for decision-making.

- Identifies trends, patterns, and anomalies.
- Communicates insights effectively to stakeholders.

17.2 Common Business Use Cases

1. **Sales**: Track revenue, product performance, and customer segments.
2. **Marketing**: Analyze campaign performance and customer engagement.
3. **Finance**: Monitor budgets, expenses, and profitability.

Section 2: Sales Data Visualization

17.3 Sales Trends Over Time

- **Line   Chart   for   Sales   Trends:
  Code Example:**

python

```
import pandas as pd
import matplotlib.pyplot as plt

# Sample data
sales_data = pd.DataFrame({
    "Month": ["Jan", "Feb", "Mar", "Apr", "May"],
    "Sales": [200, 220, 250, 300, 350]
```

```
})
```

```
plt.plot(sales_data["Month"], sales_data["Sales"], marker="o")
plt.title("Monthly Sales Trend")
plt.xlabel("Month")
plt.ylabel("Sales")
plt.grid(True)
plt.show()
```

17.4 Comparing Product Performance

- **Bar Chart for Product Sales:
  Code Example**:

python

```
products = pd.DataFrame({
    "Product": ["A", "B", "C"],
    "Sales": [500, 700, 300]
})
```

```
products.plot(kind="bar", x="Product", y="Sales", legend=False,
color="skyblue")
plt.title("Product Sales Comparison")
plt.ylabel("Sales")
plt.show()
```

Section 3: Marketing Data Visualization

17.5 Campaign Performance

- **Stacked Bar Chart for Campaign Results**: **Code Example**:

python

```python
campaigns = pd.DataFrame({
    "Channel": ["Email", "Social Media", "Search Ads"],
    "Clicks": [300, 500, 400],
    "Conversions": [50, 100, 80]
})

campaigns.plot(kind="bar", x="Channel", stacked=True,
title="Campaign Performance", color=["lightblue", "green"])
plt.ylabel("Count")
plt.show()
```

17.6 Customer Segmentation

- **Pie Chart for Customer Demographics**: **Code Example**:

python

```python
demographics = pd.DataFrame({
    "Segment": ["Youth", "Adults", "Seniors"],
    "Percentage": [40, 50, 10]
})
```

```python
plt.pie(demographics["Percentage"], labels=demographics["Segment"],
autopct="%1.1f%%", startangle=90, colors=["lightblue", "orange",
"green"])
plt.title("Customer Demographics")
plt.show()
```

Section 4: Financial Data Visualization

17.7 Budget Tracking

- **Area Chart for Budget vs. Expenses:**
  Code Example:

python

```python
budget_data = pd.DataFrame({
    "Month": ["Jan", "Feb", "Mar", "Apr", "May"],
    "Budget": [300, 320, 340, 360, 380],
    "Expenses": [280, 310, 330, 350, 370]
})
```

```python
plt.fill_between(budget_data["Month"],          budget_data["Budget"],
alpha=0.4, label="Budget", color="green")
plt.fill_between(budget_data["Month"],          budget_data["Expenses"],
alpha=0.4, label="Expenses", color="red")
plt.title("Budget vs. Expenses")
plt.legend()
plt.show()
```

17.8 Profitability Analysis

- **Box   Plot   for   Profit   Distribution**:
  Code Example:

  python

```
profits = pd.DataFrame({
    "Region": ["North", "South", "East", "West"],
    "Profit": [5000, 7000, 3000, 4000]
})

profits.boxplot(column="Profit", by="Region")
plt.title("Profit Distribution by Region")
plt.suptitle("")
plt.ylabel("Profit")
plt.show()
```

Section 5: Advanced Business Visualization with Plotly

17.9 Interactive Sales Dashboard

- Combine multiple charts in one interactive view.
- **Code Example**:

  python

```
import plotly.express as px
```

```
sales_data = pd.DataFrame({
    "Month": ["Jan", "Feb", "Mar", "Apr", "May"],
    "Sales": [200, 220, 250, 300, 350]
})

fig = px.line(sales_data, x="Month", y="Sales", title="Interactive Sales Trend")
fig.show()
```

17.10 Regional Sales Heatmap

- Visualize sales performance across geographic regions.
- **Code Example**:

python

```
import plotly.express as px

region_data = pd.DataFrame({
    "Region": ["North", "South", "East", "West"],
    "Sales": [200, 400, 300, 500]
})

fig = px.treemap(region_data, path=["Region"], values="Sales", title="Regional Sales Heatmap")
fig.show()
```

Section 6: Case Study – Business Insights Dashboard

17.11 Dataset: Company Sales and Marketing Data

1. Create a dashboard with the following:
   o   Sales trends by product and region.
   o   Marketing campaign performance metrics.
   o   Budget vs. expense analysis.
2. Use both static charts (Matplotlib) and interactive visuals (Plotly).

Chapter Summary

- Business data visualization provides actionable insights for sales, marketing, and finance.
- Use Matplotlib and Seaborn for static visuals, and Plotly for interactive dashboards.
- Tailor visuals to the needs of business stakeholders to drive informed decisions.

Exercise: Build a Business Visualization

1. Use a dataset with sales, marketing, or finance data.
2. Create at least three different visualizations (e.g., sales trends, campaign performance, budget tracking).

3. Combine static and interactive visuals for maximum impact.

4. Reflect: How do these visualizations support business decision-making?

Chapter 18: Scientific Data Visualization

Overview

Scientific data visualization is essential for analyzing, interpreting, and presenting research findings effectively. This chapter focuses on creating visuals tailored for scientific data, using Python libraries like Matplotlib, Seaborn, and Plotly. It covers techniques to ensure accuracy, clarity, and accessibility for research and academic presentations.

Key Objectives

By the end of this chapter, readers will:

1. Understand the principles of visualizing scientific data.
2. Learn to create various scientific plots, including error bars, heatmaps, and 3D plots.
3. Use Python libraries to create publication-quality and interactive scientific visuals.

Section 1: Principles of Scientific Data Visualization

18.1 Why Visualize Scientific Data?

- Simplifies complex data for analysis and presentation.

- Highlights patterns, anomalies, and relationships.
- Communicates findings to diverse audiences, including peers, stakeholders, and the public.

18.2 Key Principles

1. **Accuracy**: Avoid misleading scales or visual distortions.
2. **Clarity**: Use appropriate colors, labels, and legends.
3. **Reproducibility**: Ensure the visual can be recreated with the same data.

Section 2: Essential Plots for Scientific Data

18.3 Line Plots with Error Bars

- Used to show trends with associated uncertainty.
- **Code Example (Matplotlib)**:

python

```
import matplotlib.pyplot as plt
import numpy as np

x = np.linspace(0, 10, 10)
y = np.sin(x)
error = 0.1 + 0.1 * np.sqrt(x)
```

```
plt.errorbar(x, y, yerr=error, fmt='-o', capsize=5)
plt.title("Line Plot with Error Bars")
plt.xlabel("X-axis")
plt.ylabel("Y-axis")
plt.grid(True)
plt.show()
```

18.4 Heatmaps for Data Intensity

- Visualize relationships between variables or regions.
- **Code Example (Seaborn)**:

```python
python

import seaborn as sns
import numpy as np

data = np.random.rand(10, 10)
sns.heatmap(data, annot=True, cmap="viridis")
plt.title("Heatmap Example")
plt.show()
```

18.5 Scatter Plots with Regression Lines

- Highlight relationships between variables.
- **Code Example (Seaborn)**:

```python
python

import pandas as pd
```

```
df = pd.DataFrame({"X": [1, 2, 3, 4, 5], "Y": [1.1, 1.9, 3.0, 4.1, 5.2]})
sns.regplot(x="X", y="Y", data=df, ci=95)
plt.title("Scatter Plot with Regression Line")
plt.show()
```

Section 3: Advanced Scientific Plots

18.6 Contour Plots

- Represent three-dimensional data in two dimensions.
- **Code Example (Matplotlib)**:

    python

```
x = np.linspace(-3, 3, 100)
y = np.linspace(-3, 3, 100)
X, Y = np.meshgrid(x, y)
Z = np.sin(np.sqrt(X**2 + Y**2))

plt.contourf(X, Y, Z, cmap="coolwarm")
plt.colorbar(label="Z-value")
plt.title("Contour Plot Example")
plt.xlabel("X-axis")
plt.ylabel("Y-axis")
plt.show()
```

18.7 3D Surface Plots

- Visualize complex spatial data.

- **Code Example (Matplotlib)**:

python

```
from mpl_toolkits.mplot3d import Axes3D

fig = plt.figure()
ax = fig.add_subplot(111, projection='3d')

ax.plot_surface(X, Y, Z, cmap="viridis")
ax.set_title("3D Surface Plot")
ax.set_xlabel("X-axis")
ax.set_ylabel("Y-axis")
ax.set_zlabel("Z-axis")

plt.show()
```

Section 4: Interactive Scientific Visualizations

18.8 Interactive 3D Plots

- Create interactive visualizations with Plotly.
- **Code Example (Plotly)**:

python

```
import plotly.graph_objects as go

fig = go.Figure(data=[go.Surface(z=Z, x=X[0], y=Y[:, 0])])
```

```
fig.update_layout(title="Interactive     3D     Surface     Plot",
scene=dict(xaxis_title="X", yaxis_title="Y", zaxis_title="Z"))
fig.show()
```

18.9 Time-Series Animations

- Visualize changes in data over time.
- **Code Example (Plotly Express)**:

python

```python
import plotly.express as px
import pandas as pd

df = pd.DataFrame({
    "Time": [1, 2, 3, 4, 5],
    "Value": [10, 12, 15, 13, 17],
    "Category": ["A", "A", "B", "B", "A"]
})

fig = px.line(df, x="Time", y="Value", color="Category", title="Time-Series Animation", animation_frame="Time")
fig.show()
```

Section 5: Customizing Scientific Visualizations

18.10 Publication-Quality Visuals

- Use consistent color schemes, grid lines, and clear labels for scientific journals.
- **Code Example (Matplotlib)**:

python

```
plt.plot(x, y, label="Data")
plt.title("Publication-Quality Plot", fontsize=14)
plt.xlabel("X-axis", fontsize=12)
plt.ylabel("Y-axis", fontsize=12)
plt.legend()
plt.grid(True)
plt.show()
```

18.11 Interactive Dashboards for Research

- Combine multiple scientific visualizations into a dashboard.
- **Code Example (Streamlit)**:

python

```
import streamlit as st
st.title("Scientific Data Dashboard")
st.line_chart(df)
st.area_chart(data)
```

Section 6: Case Study – Visualizing Climate Change Data

18.12 Dataset: Global Temperature Anomalies

1. Load a dataset with temperature anomalies over decades.
2. Create:
    o Line plot with error bars for global trends.
    o Heatmap for regional temperature changes.
    o 3D surface plot for geographic temperature distributions.

Chapter Summary

- Scientific data visualization bridges the gap between raw data and meaningful insights.
- Use line plots, scatter plots, heatmaps, and 3D plots for clear, accurate representation.
- Python libraries like Matplotlib, Seaborn, and Plotly provide tools for creating static and interactive scientific visuals.

Exercise: Visualize a Scientific Dataset

1. Choose a dataset (e.g., environmental, biological, or physical science data).
2. Create three visualizations:
    o A trend line with error bars.
    o A heatmap to show intensity or correlation.

      o   A 3D surface or contour plot.

3. Reflect: How do these visuals help in analyzing and communicating the data?

Chapter 19: Social Media and Web Analytics Visualizations

Overview

Social media and web analytics play a crucial role in understanding audience behavior, measuring campaign performance, and optimizing online strategies. This chapter focuses on analyzing and visualizing key metrics from platforms like social media, websites, and online campaigns using Python libraries like Matplotlib, Seaborn, and Plotly.

Key Objectives

By the end of this chapter, readers will:

1. Understand key social media and web analytics metrics.
2. Learn to visualize engagement, traffic, and performance data.
3. Use Python libraries to create insightful and interactive analytics dashboards.

Section 1: Key Metrics in Social Media and Web Analytics

19.1 Social Media Metrics

- **Engagement**: Likes, shares, comments, and followers.
- **Reach**: Number of unique users who saw the content.
- **Click-Through Rate (CTR)**: Ratio of clicks to impressions.
- **Sentiment**: Positive, neutral, or negative feedback.

19.2 Web Analytics Metrics

- **Traffic**: Total visits, unique visitors, and bounce rate.
- **Behavior**: Average session duration, pages per session.
- **Conversions**: Goal completions or sales.
- **Acquisition**: Sources of traffic (organic, paid, referral, etc.).

Section 2: Visualizing Social Media Metrics

19.3 Engagement Over Time

- **Line Chart for Engagement Trends**: **Code Example**:

python

```
import pandas as pd
import matplotlib.pyplot as plt

data = pd.DataFrame({
    "Date": ["2023-01-01", "2023-01-02", "2023-01-03", "2023-01-04"],
    "Likes": [100, 150, 120, 180],
```

```
    "Comments": [20, 30, 25, 35]
})
```

```
plt.plot(data["Date"], data["Likes"], label="Likes", marker="o")
plt.plot(data["Date"],     data["Comments"],     label="Comments",
marker="o")
plt.title("Social Media Engagement Over Time")
plt.xlabel("Date")
plt.ylabel("Engagement")
plt.legend()
plt.grid(True)
plt.show()
```

19.4 Post Performance Comparison

- **Bar   Chart   for   Post   Metrics:**
  Code Example:

python

```
posts = pd.DataFrame({
    "Post": ["Post 1", "Post 2", "Post 3"],
    "Likes": [120, 200, 150],
    "Shares": [30, 50, 40]
})
```

```
posts.plot(kind="bar",     x="Post",     stacked=True,     title="Post
Performance", color=["skyblue", "green"])
plt.ylabel("Count")
plt.show()
```

19.5 Sentiment Analysis

- **Pie Chart for Sentiment Distribution**: **Code Example**:

python

```python
sentiment = pd.DataFrame({
    "Sentiment": ["Positive", "Neutral", "Negative"],
    "Percentage": [60, 25, 15]
})

plt.pie(sentiment["Percentage"],        labels=sentiment["Sentiment"],
autopct="%1.1f%%", startangle=90, colors=["green", "blue", "red"])
plt.title("Sentiment Analysis")
plt.show()
```

Section 3: Visualizing Web Analytics Metrics

19.6 Traffic Sources

- **Pie Chart for Traffic Acquisition**: **Code Example**:

python

```python
sources = pd.DataFrame({
    "Source": ["Organic", "Paid", "Referral", "Direct"],
    "Traffic": [500, 300, 200, 400]
```

```
})
```

```
plt.pie(sources["Traffic"],                    labels=sources["Source"],
autopct="%1.1f%%",  startangle=90,  colors=["lightblue",  "orange",
"green", "red"])
plt.title("Traffic Sources")
plt.show()
```

19.7 Bounce Rate vs. Session Duration

- **Scatter   Plot   for   Behavior   Metrics**:
  Code Example:

  python

```
behavior = pd.DataFrame({
    "BounceRate": [50, 40, 60, 45],
    "SessionDuration": [2.5, 3.0, 1.8, 2.7]
})
```

```
plt.scatter(behavior["BounceRate"],      behavior["SessionDuration"],
color="purple")
plt.title("Bounce Rate vs. Session Duration")
plt.xlabel("Bounce Rate (%)")
plt.ylabel("Session Duration (min)")
plt.grid(True)
plt.show()
```

Section 4: Advanced Visualizations for Social Media and Web Analytics

19.8 Heatmap for Page Performance

- Visualize which pages attract the most traffic.
- **Code Example (Seaborn)**:

python

```python
import seaborn as sns

data = pd.DataFrame({
    "Page": ["Home", "About", "Products", "Contact"],
    "Week1": [200, 50, 300, 100],
    "Week2": [220, 60, 320, 120],
    "Week3": [250, 70, 350, 150]
}).set_index("Page")

sns.heatmap(data, annot=True, cmap="coolwarm", fmt="d")
plt.title("Page Performance Over Time")
plt.show()
```

19.9 Interactive Social Media Dashboard

- Use Plotly to create a dynamic dashboard.
- **Code Example**:

python

```
import plotly.express as px

data = pd.DataFrame({
    "Date": ["2023-01-01", "2023-01-02", "2023-01-03"],
    "Likes": [100, 150, 200],
    "Shares": [30, 50, 70]
})

fig = px.line(data, x="Date", y=["Likes", "Shares"], title="Social Media
Engagement")
fig.show()
```

Section 5: Case Study – Social Media Campaign Dashboard

19.10 Dataset: Multi-Platform Social Media Metrics

1. **Goals**:

    o   Track performance across platforms like Facebook, Instagram, and Twitter.

    o   Visualize engagement trends, sentiment analysis, and traffic sources.

2. **Steps**:

    o   Create stacked bar charts for platform engagement.

    o   Build interactive line charts for campaign trends.

    o   Use a heatmap for performance by post type.

Chapter Summary

- Visualizing social media and web analytics helps businesses understand audience behavior and campaign effectiveness.
- Use line charts, bar charts, and scatter plots for key metrics.
- Plotly enables dynamic and interactive dashboards for deeper insights.

Exercise: Build a Social Media Dashboard

1. Use a dataset with engagement metrics (e.g., likes, shares, comments) across platforms.
2. Create at least three visualizations:
   o Engagement trends over time.
   o Post performance comparison.
   o Traffic source distribution.
3. Reflect: How do these visualizations support decision-making for marketing strategies?

Chapter 20: Health and Epidemiological Data Visualization

Overview

Visualizing health and epidemiological data is essential for tracking diseases, analyzing health trends, and informing policy decisions. This chapter focuses on creating clear and actionable visuals for health data, using Python libraries like Matplotlib, Seaborn, and Plotly. Examples include tracking infections, visualizing vaccination rates, and analyzing healthcare resource utilization.

Key Objectives

By the end of this chapter, readers will:

1. Understand the importance of visualizing health and epidemiological data.
2. Learn to create various health-focused visualizations.
3. Use Python libraries to produce clear and informative visuals for health-related datasets.

Section 1: Importance of Health Data Visualization

20.1 Why Visualize Health Data?

- Communicates complex information effectively to stakeholders, policymakers, and the public.
- Highlights trends, patterns, and disparities in health outcomes.
- Supports decision-making in public health and healthcare resource allocation.

20.2 Common Health Metrics

- **Disease Trends**: Infection rates, mortality rates, recovery rates.
- **Healthcare Resources**: Hospital beds, ICU usage, vaccination coverage.
- **Demographics**: Age, gender, and geographic distribution of health outcomes.

Section 2: Visualizing Epidemiological Data

20.3 Disease Incidence Over Time

- **Line Chart for Infection Trends: Code Example**:

python

```
import pandas as pd
```

```
import matplotlib.pyplot as plt

data = pd.DataFrame({
    "Date": ["2023-01-01", "2023-01-02", "2023-01-03", "2023-01-04"],
    "Infections": [100, 150, 200, 300]
})

plt.plot(data["Date"], data["Infections"], marker="o", label="Infections")
plt.title("Daily Infection Trends")
plt.xlabel("Date")
plt.ylabel("Infections")
plt.grid(True)
plt.legend()
plt.show()
```

20.4 Geographical Distribution of Cases

- **Choropleth Map for Case Distribution: Code Example (Plotly)**:

python

```
import plotly.express as px

data = pd.DataFrame({
    "Country": ["USA", "India", "Brazil"],
    "Cases": [1000000, 800000, 700000]
})
```

```python
fig = px.choropleth(data, locations="Country", locationmode="country
names", color="Cases",
                title="COVID-19        Case        Distribution",
color_continuous_scale="Reds")
fig.show()
```

Section 3: Visualizing Healthcare Resource Data

20.5 ICU and Bed Utilization

- **Stacked Bar Chart for Resource Allocation**:
  Code Example:

  python

  ```python
  resources = pd.DataFrame({
      "Hospital": ["A", "B", "C"],
      "ICU Beds Used": [50, 70, 40],
      "General Beds Used": [200, 300, 150]
  })

  resources.plot(kind="bar",        x="Hospital",        stacked=True,
  title="Healthcare Resource Utilization", color=["red", "blue"])
  plt.ylabel("Beds Used")
  plt.show()
  ```

20.6 Vaccination Progress

- **Gauge Chart for Vaccination Rates:
  Code Example (Plotly)**:

  python

  ```
  import plotly.graph_objects as go

  fig = go.Figure(go.Indicator(
      mode="gauge+number",
      value=75,
      title={"text": "Vaccination Rate"},
      gauge={"axis": {"range": [0, 100]}, "bar": {"color": "green"}}
  ))
  fig.show()
  ```

Section 4: Advanced Visualizations for Health Data

20.7 Heatmaps for Disease Correlations

- Visualize relationships between symptoms or conditions.
- **Code Example (Seaborn)**:

  python

  ```
  import seaborn as sns
  import numpy as np

  data = np.random.rand(5, 5)
  ```

```
sns.heatmap(data,          annot=True,          cmap="coolwarm",
xticklabels=["Symptom1", "Symptom2", "Symptom3", "Symptom4",
"Symptom5"],
         yticklabels=["Symptom1",     "Symptom2",     "Symptom3",
"Symptom4", "Symptom5"])
plt.title("Symptom Correlation Heatmap")
plt.show()
```

20.8 Time-Series Animations for Epidemics

- Visualize the spread of infections over time.
- **Code Example (Plotly Express)**:

python

```
data = pd.DataFrame({
    "Date": ["2023-01-01", "2023-01-02", "2023-01-03"],
    "Country": ["USA", "USA", "USA"],
    "Cases": [100, 300, 600]
})

fig = px.bar(data, x="Date", y="Cases", animation_frame="Date",
title="Infection Spread Over Time")
fig.show()
```

Section 5: Case Study – COVID-19 Dashboard

20.9 Dataset: COVID-19 Metrics by Country and Date

1. Visualize infection trends with a line chart.

2. Map case distribution with a choropleth.

3. Create a stacked bar chart for healthcare resource utilization.

4. Build an interactive dashboard with multiple components.

Chapter Summary

- Health and epidemiological data visualization enables tracking, analysis, and communication of critical health metrics.

- Use line charts, choropleth maps, and stacked bar charts for static and interactive representations.

- Python libraries like Matplotlib, Seaborn, and Plotly simplify the creation of impactful health visuals.

Exercise: Create a Health Data Visualization

1. Choose a dataset (e.g., disease trends, vaccination rates, or healthcare resource utilization).

2. Create at least three visualizations:

   o A line chart for trends over time.

   o A choropleth map for geographic distribution.

   o A stacked bar chart for resource utilization.

3. Reflect: How do these visuals support understanding and decision-making in public health?

Chapter 21: Environmental and Climate Data Visualizations

Overview

Visualizing environmental and climate data helps uncover patterns, assess risks, and communicate scientific findings to stakeholders and the public. This chapter focuses on creating compelling and actionable visuals to analyze temperature trends, CO_2 emissions, biodiversity, and other environmental metrics using Python libraries like Matplotlib, Seaborn, and Plotly.

Key Objectives

By the end of this chapter, readers will:

1. Understand the importance of visualizing environmental and climate data.
2. Learn to create various environmental visualizations, including time-series trends, heatmaps, and geographic data.
3. Use Python libraries to communicate complex climate data effectively.

Section 1: The Importance of Environmental Data Visualization

21.1 Why Visualize Environmental Data?

- Communicates the urgency of environmental challenges.
- Aids in decision-making for sustainability and conservation.
- Reveals long-term trends and patterns in climate and biodiversity.

21.2 Common Environmental Metrics

1. **Climate**: Temperature anomalies, CO2 levels, sea level rise.
2. **Pollution**: Air quality index, emissions, waste generation.
3. **Ecosystems**: Deforestation rates, biodiversity loss.

Section 2: Visualizing Climate Data

21.3 Global Temperature Trends

- **Line Chart for Temperature Anomalies: Code Example (Matplotlib)**:

  python

  ```
  import pandas as pd
  import matplotlib.pyplot as plt
  ```

```
data = pd.DataFrame({
    "Year": [2000, 2005, 2010, 2015, 2020],
    "Temperature Anomaly": [0.2, 0.3, 0.5, 0.8, 1.0]
})
```

```
plt.plot(data["Year"], data["Temperature Anomaly"], marker="o",
label="Anomaly")
plt.title("Global Temperature Anomalies Over Time")
plt.xlabel("Year")
plt.ylabel("Temperature Anomaly (°C)")
plt.grid(True)
plt.legend()
plt.show()
```

21.4 CO2 Emissions by Country

- **Bar Chart for Emissions Comparison**: **Code Example (Matplotlib)**:

python

```
emissions = pd.DataFrame({
    "Country": ["USA", "China", "India", "EU"],
    "CO2 Emissions": [5000, 10000, 2500, 4000]
})
```

```
emissions.plot(kind="bar", x="Country", y="CO2 Emissions",
color="red", legend=False)
plt.title("CO2 Emissions by Country")
```

```
plt.ylabel("CO2 Emissions (Million Metric Tons)")
plt.show()
```

Section 3: Geographic and Spatial Visualizations

21.5 Mapping Deforestation Rates

- **Choropleth Map for Forest Cover Change**: **Code Example (Plotly)**:

python

```python
import plotly.express as px

data = pd.DataFrame({
    "Country": ["Brazil", "Indonesia", "Congo"],
    "Deforestation Rate": [-0.5, -0.3, -0.2]
})

fig = px.choropleth(data, locations="Country", locationmode="country names", color="Deforestation Rate",
            title="Deforestation      Rates      by      Country",
color_continuous_scale="YlGn")
fig.show()
```

21.6 Air Quality Index Heatmap

- **Heatmap for Air Pollution Levels**: **Code Example (Seaborn)**:

python

```
import seaborn as sns
import numpy as np

data = np.random.rand(10, 10)
sns.heatmap(data, annot=False, cmap="coolwarm")
plt.title("Air Quality Index Heatmap")
plt.show()
```

Section 4: Advanced Climate Visualizations

21.7 Sea Level Rise Visualization

- **Line Chart with Confidence Intervals: Code Example (Seaborn):**

python

```
data = pd.DataFrame({
    "Year": [2000, 2005, 2010, 2015, 2020],
    "Sea Level": [0.2, 0.25, 0.3, 0.4, 0.5],
    "Error": [0.02, 0.03, 0.02, 0.04, 0.03]
})

sns.lineplot(x="Year", y="Sea Level", data=data, ci="sd")
plt.title("Sea Level Rise Over Time")
plt.xlabel("Year")
plt.ylabel("Sea Level (meters)")
```

```
plt.show()
```

21.8 Interactive Visualizations of Climate Change

- **CO2 Emissions Over Time (Interactive)**: **Code Example (Plotly)**:

python

```
data = pd.DataFrame({
    "Year": [2000, 2005, 2010, 2015, 2020],
    "USA": [5000, 5200, 5400, 5500, 5600],
    "China": [6000, 8000, 9000, 10000, 12000]
})

fig = px.line(data, x="Year", y=["USA", "China"], title="CO2
Emissions Over Time", labels={"value": "Emissions", "variable":
"Country"})
fig.show()
```

Section 5: Case Study – Climate Change Dashboard

21.9 Dataset: Global Climate Metrics

1. **Goals**:

   o Visualize temperature anomalies over decades.

   o Map CO2 emissions by region.

   o Show deforestation trends and air quality metrics.

2. **Steps**:

- o Create a line chart for temperature anomalies.
- o Use a choropleth map for emissions.
- o Build a dashboard combining multiple visuals.

Chapter Summary

- Environmental and climate data visualization aids in understanding global challenges.
- Use line charts, bar charts, and geographic visualizations for impactful storytelling.
- Python libraries like Matplotlib, Seaborn, and Plotly make it easy to create static and interactive visuals.

Exercise: Create Environmental Visualizations

1. Choose a dataset (e.g., temperature trends, CO2 emissions, or deforestation rates).
2. Create three visualizations:
   - o A trend line with anomalies over time.
   - o A geographic map for spatial data.
   - o A heatmap for regional or temporal intensity.

3. Reflect: How do these visuals enhance understanding of environmental issues?

Chapter 22: Best Practices for Effective Visualizations

Overview

Creating effective visualizations requires more than technical skills—it involves understanding color theory, choosing the right chart for the data, and tailoring visuals to the audience. This chapter explores best practices for crafting clear, engaging, and meaningful visualizations that maximize impact.

Key Objectives

By the end of this chapter, readers will:

1. Understand how to use color theory effectively in data visualization.
2. Learn to choose appropriate charts based on data type and insights.
3. Tailor visualizations to meet audience needs and expectations.

Section 1: The Foundations of Effective Visualization

22.1 Why Do Visualizations Matter?

- **Communication**: Translates complex data into understandable insights.
- **Decision-Making**: Supports informed decisions in business, science, and other fields.
- **Engagement**: Captures attention and maintains interest.

22.2 The Three Pillars of Effective Visuals

1. **Accuracy**: Represent data truthfully without distortion.
2. **Clarity**: Eliminate unnecessary elements and prioritize readability.
3. **Focus**: Highlight key insights to guide the audience's attention.

Section 2: Color Theory in Data Visualization

22.3 The Role of Color

- Color enhances comprehension and highlights key data points.
- Avoid overusing color, which can overwhelm and confuse viewers.

22.4 Choosing Effective Color Palettes

- **Sequential Palettes**: For ordered data (e.g., gradients from low to high).

  o   Example: Blues, Greens.

- **Diverging Palettes**: For data with a midpoint (e.g., profit/loss).

  o   Example: RdBu, PiYG.

- **Categorical Palettes**: For distinct groups.

  o   Example: Set2, Dark2.

22.5 Avoiding Common Color Mistakes

- Avoid colors that are too similar; they reduce differentiation.
- Be mindful of colorblind-friendly palettes.
- **Code Example (Seaborn Palette)**:

python

```
import seaborn as sns
import matplotlib.pyplot as plt

sns.set_palette("colorblind")
data = [10, 20, 15, 30]
labels = ["A", "B", "C", "D"]

plt.bar(labels, data)
plt.title("Colorblind-Friendly Visualization")
plt.show()
```

Section 3: Chart Selection Based on Data Type

22.6 Matching Charts to Data

Objective	Recommended Chart
Show trends over time	Line chart, area chart
Compare categories	Bar chart, pie chart
Show relationships between variables	Scatter plot, bubble chart
Represent proportions	Pie chart, donut chart, stacked bars
Highlight distributions	Histogram, box plot

22.7 Avoiding Chart Misuse

- **Pie Charts**: Limit to 4-5 categories to maintain readability.
- **3D Charts**: Avoid unless necessary; they can distort perception.
- **Code Example for Chart Selection**:

python

```
import pandas as pd
import seaborn as sns
```

```
df = pd.DataFrame({"Category": ["A", "B", "C"], "Values": [100, 150,
200]})
sns.barplot(x="Category", y="Values", data=df)
plt.title("Category Comparison")
plt.show()
```

Section 4: Tailoring Visuals to Your Audience

22.8 Knowing Your Audience

- **General Public**: Use simple, engaging visuals with minimal text.
- **Experts**: Include detailed annotations, scales, and context.
- **Stakeholders**: Focus on actionable insights and key takeaways.

22.9 Simplifying Complex Visuals

- Use annotations to explain key data points.
- Break down complex visuals into smaller, digestible parts.
- **Code Example (Matplotlib Annotation)**:

python

import matplotlib.pyplot as plt

x = [1, 2, 3, 4, 5]
y = [10, 20, 15, 30, 25]

196

```
plt.plot(x, y, marker="o")
plt.title("Annotated Line Chart")
plt.xlabel("Time")
plt.ylabel("Value")
plt.annotate("Peak", xy=(4, 30), xytext=(3, 35),
        arrowprops=dict(facecolor="red", arrowstyle="->"))
plt.show()
```

Section 5: Enhancing Visualizations with Design Principles

22.10 Design Tips for Clear Visuals

- **Consistency**: Use uniform font sizes, colors, and styles.
- **Whitespace**: Avoid overcrowding; give elements space to breathe.
- **Alignment**: Ensure alignment of labels, axes, and legends.

22.11 Adding Context with Text and Labels

- Always include a title, axis labels, and legends.
- Use subtitles for additional context.

Section 6: Case Study – Revamping a Business Report

22.12 Dataset: Sales Performance by Region

1. **Original Chart**: A cluttered, color-heavy bar chart with too many categories.
2. **Improved Visual**:
   - Simplify categories into groups (e.g., North, South, East, West).
   - Use a sequential color palette for better clarity.
   - Add annotations for key insights (e.g., top-performing region).

Chapter Summary

- Effective visualizations require attention to color, chart type, and audience needs.
- Avoid common pitfalls like overloading visuals with unnecessary elements.
- Apply design principles to ensure clarity, accuracy, and focus.

Exercise: Apply Best Practices to Your Visualizations

1. Take an existing visualization you've created.
2. Assess it using the pillars of effective visuals (accuracy, clarity, focus).

3. Revise the visualization:

   ○ Adjust the color palette for better readability.

   ○ Ensure the chart type matches the data.

   ○ Add annotations to emphasize key points.

4. Reflect: How did these changes improve the visualization?

Chapter 23: Exporting and Sharing Your Visualizations

Overview

Creating visually appealing and informative charts is only part of the process—exporting and sharing them effectively is equally important. This chapter focuses on techniques for exporting high-quality visualizations suitable for presentations, reports, and publications, and highlights best practices for sharing visualizations across platforms.

Key Objectives

By the end of this chapter, readers will:

1. Understand how to export visualizations in high-quality formats.
2. Learn techniques for embedding visuals in reports, presentations, and web platforms.
3. Explore tools for sharing static and interactive visualizations effectively.

Section 1: Exporting High-Quality Visuals

23.1 Choosing the Right File Format

- **PNG**: High-quality raster image, suitable for presentations.
- **JPEG**: Compressed format, less ideal for charts with text.
- **SVG**: Vector format for scalable, editable graphics.
- **PDF**: Publication-quality format for print or academic use.

23.2 Exporting Static Visualizations

- **Matplotlib**: Save as PNG, SVG, or PDF. **Code Example**:

python

```
import matplotlib.pyplot as plt

x = [1, 2, 3, 4, 5]
y = [10, 20, 15, 30, 25]

plt.plot(x, y)
plt.title("Example Chart")
plt.savefig("chart.png", dpi=300, format="png")  # High resolution
plt.savefig("chart.pdf", format="pdf")        # Publication-quality
plt.show()
```

- **Seaborn**: Export with Matplotlib's savefig(). **Code Example**:

python

```
import seaborn as sns
data = [10, 20, 15, 30, 25]
sns.lineplot(x=range(len(data)), y=data)
plt.savefig("seaborn_chart.svg", format="svg")
```

23.3 Exporting Interactive Visualizations

- **Plotly**: Save as HTML or static images. **Code Example**:

python

```
import plotly.express as px

fig = px.scatter(x=[1, 2, 3], y=[4, 5, 6], title="Interactive Chart")
fig.write_html("interactive_chart.html")  # Shareable HTML
fig.write_image("chart.png")  # Requires `kaleido` for image exports
```

  o Install kaleido for exporting Plotly images:

bash

```
pip install -U kaleido
```

Section 2: Embedding Visualizations in Reports and Presentations

23.4 Including Visuals in Reports

- **Word Processors (e.g., MS Word)**: Insert PNG, SVG, or PDF for best results.
- **LaTeX**: Use EPS or PDF for embedding in academic papers. **Code Example (LaTeX)**:

```latex
\includegraphics[width=\textwidth]{chart.pdf}
```

23.5 Adding Visuals to Presentations

- Use PNG or SVG for PowerPoint or Google Slides to maintain clarity when resizing.
- Include animations for interactive presentations: Export HTML or GIFs for dynamic effects.

Section 3: Sharing Visualizations on Web Platforms

23.6 Sharing Static Visualizations

- Upload high-resolution PNG or SVG files to social media, blogs, or websites.
- Optimize file sizes for faster loading without sacrificing quality.
  - Use tools like TinyPNG for compression.

23.7 Sharing Interactive Visualizations

- Host interactive charts on platforms like:
  - **GitHub Pages**: Share HTML files.
  - **Streamlit Sharing**: Deploy dashboards and interactive apps.
  - **Tableau Public**: Publish visualizations for public access.

Section 4: Ensuring Visual Accessibility

23.8 Colorblind-Friendly Visuals

- Use accessible color palettes like colorblind in Seaborn or Plotly.

23.9 Adding Descriptive Alt Text

- Provide meaningful descriptions for accessibility:
  - Example: *"Line chart showing revenue growth from 2015 to 2020, with a steady upward trend."*

Section 5: Case Study – Preparing a Visualization for Multiple Platforms

23.10 Dataset: Sales Performance by Region

1. Create a bar chart visualizing regional sales using Matplotlib.
2. Save the chart as:
   - PNG for a PowerPoint presentation.
   - PDF for an academic report.
   - HTML for embedding on a company website.
3. Optimize the file size for web use.

Chapter Summary

- Exporting and sharing visualizations ensures your insights reach the intended audience effectively.
- Use appropriate formats for presentations, publications, and web sharing.
- Consider accessibility and optimize files for quality and performance.

Exercise: Practice Exporting and Sharing Visualizations

1. Create a visualization (e.g., line chart, bar chart) using Matplotlib, Seaborn, or Plotly.
2. Export the visualization as:
   o   PNG for a presentation.
   o   PDF for a publication.
   o   HTML for web sharing.
3. Share the visualization and gather feedback on its clarity and quality.

Chapter 24: Troubleshooting and Debugging Visualization Code

Overview

Even the most experienced data visualizers encounter challenges while creating charts. This chapter addresses common issues in data visualization projects and provides solutions for troubleshooting and debugging. Topics include dealing with data mismatches, resolving display errors, and optimizing visuals for performance.

Key Objectives

By the end of this chapter, readers will:

1. Identify and resolve common errors in data visualization code.
2. Understand debugging techniques specific to Matplotlib, Seaborn, and Plotly.
3. Learn to optimize code for efficient and error-free visualizations.

Section 1: Common Visualization Issues and Solutions

24.1 Data Mismatches

- **Issue**: Data dimensions don't match the chart type (e.g., X and Y arrays have different lengths). **Solution**: Check data shapes and align dimensions. **Code Example**:

```python

import numpy as np
import matplotlib.pyplot as plt


x = np.array([1, 2, 3])
y = np.array([4, 5])  # Mismatched length

# Fix:
if len(x) != len(y):
    print("Error: X and Y must have the same length.")
```

24.2 Incorrect Chart Types

- **Issue**: Using an inappropriate chart type for the data (e.g., a bar chart for continuous data). **Solution**: Choose a chart type that aligns with the data type.

24.3 Overlapping Elements

- **Issue**: Legends, labels, or annotations overlap with the plot area. **Solution**: Adjust layout or use padding. **Code Example (Matplotlib)**:

python

plt.tight_layout() # Automatically adjusts spacing

24.4 Performance Issues with Large Datasets

- **Issue**: Visualizations with large datasets become slow or unresponsive.
  Solution: Downsample or aggregate the data before plotting.
  Code Example:

python

```
import pandas as pd

data = pd.DataFrame({"x": range(1000000), "y": range(1000000)})
sampled_data = data.sample(1000)  # Downsample to 1,000 points
```

24.5 Plot Display Errors

- **Issue**: Charts don't render in Jupyter Notebook or certain environments.
  Solution: Ensure required backends are loaded.
  Code Example (Jupyter Notebook):

python

```
%matplotlib inline
```

Section 2: Debugging Matplotlib Visualizations

24.6 Check for Missing Data

- **Issue**: Gaps or unexpected behavior due to missing values.
  Solution: Remove or fill missing data before plotting.
  Code Example:

  python

  ```
  import pandas as pd

  data = pd.DataFrame({"x": [1, 2, None, 4], "y": [10, 20, 30, 40]})
  data = data.dropna()  # Remove rows with missing values
  ```

24.7 Analyzing Axes and Limits

- **Issue**: Plots appear empty due to incorrect axis limits.
  Solution: Check   and   adjust   limits.
  Code Example:

  python

  ```
  plt.xlim(0, 10)
  plt.ylim(0, 100)
  ```

Section 3: Debugging Seaborn Visualizations

24.8 Palette Errors

- **Issue**: Unsupported color palettes or mismatched colors. **Solution**: Use a valid Seaborn palette. **Code Example**:

```python
import seaborn as sns

sns.set_palette("viridis")
sns.barplot(x=["A", "B", "C"], y=[1, 2, 3])
plt.show()
```

24.9 Data Misalignment in Seaborn

- **Issue**: Seaborn relies heavily on Pandas DataFrames; raw arrays may cause errors. **Solution**: Ensure data is properly formatted as a DataFrame.

Section 4: Debugging Plotly Visualizations

24.10 Missing Dependencies for Export

- **Issue**: Plotly fails to export images (e.g., PNG). **Solution**: Install the required kaleido library. **Command**:

```bash
```

```
pip install kaleido
```

24.11 Interactive Plot Issues

- **Issue**: Interactive plots don't render in Jupyter Notebook. **Solution**: Use the correct renderer. **Code Example**:

```python
python

import plotly.io as pio

pio.renderers.default = "notebook"  # Use notebook renderer
```

Section 5: Optimization Techniques for Efficient Visualizations

24.12 Avoid Overplotting

- For large datasets, simplify by aggregating data or using transparency.
- **Code Example (Scatter Plot with Transparency)**:

```python
python

plt.scatter(x, y, alpha=0.5)
```

24.13 Use Efficient Libraries for Big Data

- Libraries like Datashader and Holoviews handle large datasets efficiently.

  Code Example (Datashader):

  python

  ```python
  import datashader as ds
  import pandas as pd

  df = pd.DataFrame({"x": range(100000), "y": range(100000)})
  canvas = ds.Canvas(plot_width=400, plot_height=400)
  agg = canvas.points(df, "x", "y")
  ```

Section 6: Case Study – Debugging a Visualization Workflow

24.14 Scenario: Analyzing Sales Trends

1. **Problem**: A line chart of sales over time appears blank.
2. **Issues Found**:
   o Missing values in the dataset.
   o Axis limits are outside the data range.
3. **Steps Taken**:
   o Cleaned data by filling missing values.
   o Adjusted axis limits to match the data.

Chapter Summary

- Debugging visualization code involves identifying data mismatches, correcting errors in chart configurations, and optimizing performance.
- Tools like Matplotlib, Seaborn, and Plotly offer solutions for common issues, but understanding data structure and visualization principles is key.
- Optimize visualizations for large datasets using techniques like downsampling or leveraging efficient libraries.

Exercise: Troubleshoot a Visualization

1. Create a visualization with intentional errors (e.g., missing data, mismatched dimensions).
2. Identify the issues using debugging techniques.
3. Resolve the errors and produce a correct visualization.
4. Reflect: What debugging steps were most useful in resolving the issues?

Chapter 25: Emerging Trends and Tools in Data Visualization

Overview

The field of data visualization is rapidly evolving, driven by advances in artificial intelligence (AI), augmented reality (AR), virtual reality (VR), and real-time analytics. This chapter explores emerging trends and tools shaping the future of data visualization, enabling readers to stay ahead of the curve in presenting data effectively and innovatively.

Key Objectives

By the end of this chapter, readers will:

1. Understand the latest trends in data visualization.
2. Explore AI-powered tools for automated insights and visualization.
3. Learn about immersive technologies like AR and VR for dynamic data representation.

Section 1: Emerging Trends in Data Visualization

25.1 AI-Powered Visualization Tools

- **Trend**: Tools like Tableau, Power BI, and Google Data Studio are integrating AI for:
  - **Automated Insights**: Identifying key patterns without manual effort.
  - **Natural Language Queries**: Generating charts with plain language commands.
  - **Predictive Analytics**: Visualizing future trends based on historical data.

25.2 Real-Time Data Visualization

- **Trend**: Businesses increasingly rely on real-time dashboards to track live metrics.
- **Applications**:
  - Monitoring website traffic.
  - Tracking supply chain logistics.
  - Observing stock market movements.

25.3 Immersive Visualization with AR and VR

- **Trend**: Immersive technologies enable data exploration in 3D environments.
- **Examples**:
  - Visualizing geographic data in AR for urban planning.

    o Using VR to analyze multidimensional datasets interactively.

Section 2: AI-Powered Tools and Libraries

25.4 Automated Charting Tools

- **Examples**:
  - **DataRobot**: Automated machine learning and visualization.
  - **Charticulator**: Create custom visuals without coding.

25.5 Python Libraries Integrating AI

- **Plotly Express with AI Features**: Generates recommendations for chart types based on data. **Code Example**:

```python
python

import plotly.express as px
import pandas as pd

df = pd.DataFrame({"Category": ["A", "B", "C"], "Values": [100, 150, 200]})
```

```
fig = px.bar(df, x="Category", y="Values", title="AI-Recommended
Chart")
fig.show()
```

Section 3: Augmented Reality and Virtual Reality in Visualization

25.6 AR Applications

- Overlay data on real-world environments using devices like smartphones or AR glasses.
- **Tools**:
    - **Microsoft HoloLens**: Visualize business metrics in 3D.
    - **Google ARCore**: Create AR-based data interactions.

25.7 VR Applications

- Immersive environments allow users to "walk through" datasets.
- **Tools**:
    - **Unity3D with Python**: Integrate Python data processing with VR development.
    - **Vizard**: Specialized VR development platform for research and analytics.

Section 4: Interactive and Multidimensional Visualizations

25.8 Multidimensional Data Exploration

- Explore datasets with multiple variables interactively.
- **Code Example (Plotly 3D Scatter Plot)**:

python

```python
import plotly.graph_objects as go

fig = go.Figure(data=[go.Scatter3d(
    x=[1, 2, 3], y=[4, 5, 6], z=[7, 8, 9],
    mode="markers",
    marker=dict(size=10, color=[7, 8, 9], colorscale="Viridis")
)])
fig.update_layout(title="3D Data Exploration")
fig.show()
```

25.9 Gesture-Based Interactions

- Future systems may use hand gestures for filtering, zooming, and manipulating visuals.

Section 5: Sustainability and Ethical Visualization

25.10 Green Visualizations

- Minimizing the energy footprint of computationally expensive visualizations.
- Emphasizing the role of visualization in addressing environmental challenges.

25.11 Ethical Data Representation

- Avoiding manipulation or bias in visualized data.
- Tools for validating and auditing visualizations for accuracy.

Section 6: Preparing for the Future

25.12 Skillsets for the Future

- **Coding + Design**: Merging programming with aesthetic visualization skills.
- **AR/VR Development**: Learning tools like Unity, Unreal Engine, and WebXR.
- **AI Integration**: Using Python libraries like TensorFlow or PyTorch to combine analytics with visualization.

25.13 Learning Resources

- Online platforms like Coursera and Udemy offer specialized courses in modern visualization techniques.

Section 7: Case Study – Designing the Future Dashboard

25.14 Dataset: Real-Time Environmental Metrics

1. Combine live data feeds (e.g., air quality, temperature) with AI-powered insights.
2. Create a dashboard with interactive and immersive visualizations using Plotly.
3. Use AR tools to overlay environmental data on real-world maps.

Chapter Summary

- The future of data visualization is driven by AI, real-time analytics, and immersive technologies like AR and VR.
- Python remains a core tool, with libraries like Plotly and emerging frameworks integrating cutting-edge features.
- Preparing for these trends involves acquiring skills in AI, AR, and ethical visualization practices.

Exercise: Explore Emerging Visualization Trends

1. Create a 3D scatter plot or heatmap using Plotly or Matplotlib.

2. Research an AI-powered visualization tool and try a basic project.

3. Reflect: How do emerging technologies enhance data storytelling?